AUTHOR'S NOTE

For this reprint I wish to make it clear that the Game of "Soro" (pages 44 to 46 and references under Contents and in the Vocabulary) is more than a game, and I had thought to replace "game", wherever it appears in connection with Soro, by "ceremony": but "ceremony" seems to imply solemnity, as also does "rite" or "ritual"; and a Soro gathering is anything but solemn — it is a very lively affair indeed. I therefore think it better to retain "game" and ask the reader to visualise "Soro" as "the observance of a customary rite carried out in the spirit of a game".

I now make two additions to this section. On page 45, lines 12-13 are to read, "On the last day, *or on a subsequent occasion*, he revenges himself . . ." On page 46 the following paragraph is to be added to the section, "The series of tests eventually proves the virility of the participator and his worthiness as a member of the kin when passing from family to clan authority, independent of his parents, with an establishment of his own. Thus, in the wider sense, "Soro" indicates the change of habits and status involved during participation in the tests over a period of several years from the time of puberty to young manhood, often effecting confirmation of childhood betrothal which had been agreed between parents or influencing choice of a husband by a girl of marriageable age at this time".

Bauchi,
North-Eastern state,
Nigeria

May 1971 F.W. de ST CROIX

The Fulani of Northern Nigeria

Some General Notes

by

F. W. de St Croix

MBE., DIP. AGRIC.

NORTHERN REGION OF NIGERIA, VETERINARY DEPT. 1927-1951
AND RURAL EDUCATION, MINISTRY OF EDUCATION 1951-1961

WITH A NOTE BY THE
AUTHOR

1972

GREGG INTERNATIONAL PUBLISHERS LIMITED

ISBN 0 576 17120 4

Republished in 1972 by Gregg International Publishers Limited
Westmead, Farnborough, Hants, England

Printed in England

CONTENTS

Some General Notes on the Fulani of Northern Nigeria

HISTORY

TO anyone who has cared to follow up what little is known of the history of Fulani from early times, it appears evident that there were wide differences in status in their civilisation.

Tradition is strong that Fulani originated somewhere " to the East " ; but historically it appears that early during the thirteenth century Fulani immigrated to the Hausa states and Bornu from the West — probably owing to some threat to their independence, demands for tribute, or the like.

We are told of Fulani preachers of the doctrines of Islam in Bornu and in the Hausa states. Also of a nomadic class caring only for its herds and flocks ; holding itself strictly aloof from other races ; retaining to the full its racial characteristics and customs : herdsmen who cared little for religion and nothing for power ; but wholly for their livestock : they apparently paid some small tribute to the reigning chiefs.

From the fifteenth century onwards members of the learned or ' aristocratic ' class held high positions of office or rank as advisers, imams, judges, commanders of armies, and the like, in the states of the period, on account of their intellect. Besides this they formed states of their own. They became a ruling class : their independence of character appears at all times to have been acknowledged.

At this period the nomadic tribes, in their mode of living, showed a like independent spirit ; paying tribute or a grazing tax to those chiefs in whose lands they grazed their cattle ; but owing allegiance to none, and moving from territory to territory, at will, throughout the Western Sudan, from the upper reaches of the Senegal River to Lake Chad.

In the seventeenth and eighteenth centuries there were great numbers of Fulani in the Hausa states and western Bornu : each chief town had a Fulani quarter, the ruling class of Fulani having risen in position far above the herders of cattle and sheep ; intermarried with the families of the ruling negroid chiefs and, while retaining those Fulani characteristics of intellect and a capacity for administration, had lost, or were losing, their distinctive physical features and, in adopting many of the customs of the peoples with whom they merged themselves, were losing their own customs ; the language of the country in most places replaced their own. This became more pronounced with the religious revival which commenced about 1804 when, in the Hausa states, the Fulani language (Fulfulde) of the ruling class was gradually replaced by Hausa, and a social amalgamation took place ; while, in Adamawa, intermarriage and concubinage ' corrupted ' the Fulani blood, though there was no such merger as in the Hausa states, and the Fulani rulers did not abandon Fulfulde.

This religious revival followed upon the Fulani victory in what was, originally, a local fight for survival for all classes of the race against the Gobirawa; following which the Fulani leaders — men of the 'aristocratic' class — went on to exploit their success, with those people of other races who would ally themselves to them and under their leadership; and developed the religious revival into a conquest of the 'habe' rulers in order to obtain power over a great area. Apart from giving local, but yeoman, help in the initial fight for Fulani survival against the Gobirawa, it would appear that, in the subsequent movement to assume power and oust native rulers, the Nomadic Fulani took no further part.

As will appear later, this mixing of the blood of the ruling classes made even greater the gulf between them and the nomadic classes.

With both, independence and innate pride of race was, and still is, a chief characteristic. They consider all the negroid and negro races as inferior, ranking themselves as a red—or, as we should term it, white—race; negroids and negroes as black. In this connection I would note that Europeans are referred to as 'wodebe' (singular, bodejo), the red (brown) men. But the nomadic classes had in those days — and still have — maintained their age-old exclusiveness, their customs and characteristics; remain aloof, speaking their own language, uneducated, and retaining to a great extent the superstitious beliefs and fears which their forefathers held before the general spread of Islam. They describe themselves as being like birds—if one is touched, all the others fly away—an apt comparison. Their confidence is not easily gained; but may be easily lost.

During the unsettled times before the coming of the British, the Nomadic Fulani lived far from the towns in bush, usually in such large encampments that it would need a considerable force to make a successful raid on them: as skilled bowmen they were well able and, of course keen, to protect their cattle.

Of the Settled Fulani, possessors in many cases of large numbers of cattle, the owners lived within the towns. The herd was penned near the town under the charge of a trusted slave, who had slave herdsmen to assist him if cattle were numerous. There also the owner would send his sons, in turn, to take part in the work until, after they had married, some would decide to dwell in the town, others to remain on the farmland and with the flocks and herds. When the father died, the eldest son would take his place in the town, as head of the family.

In the event of a cattle raid, one or more of the party were able to escape and run to the owner with the news, whereupon he would collect a body of men to overtake the raiding party and, where possible, recapture the cattle. By living in the town there was the added advantage that, although part of the family was surprised, there was always a stronger part left to retaliate.

Then, as now, they farmed extensively, and practically all of them kept, as they still do, a number of sheep, goats and fowls. (It may be noted that Nomadic Fulani travel with their fowls and chickens.)

At the present time many towns have a Fulani village adjacent to them, or Fulani camps are found grouped about at some little distance, in their own farmlands.

As regards the relationship of the Nomadic Fulani with the rulers, it would appear that the majority of, if not all, such tribes had, from long ago, representatives of their own in the towns of the ruling chiefs. It is reasonable to agree with the Fulani assumption that this representation came about in such manner as that, as a young man, a member of a family of standing, perhaps the son of an 'ardo' (Fulani chief or leader), would decide to give up the nomadic life for that of scholarship and, having been given a wife, retire with her to a town. From time to time relatives would visit and stay with him, and exchange news: when a man of learning was required he would be called in by them. He would be given a voluntary 'fee' for his assistance, and presents would be given to him on various occasions. These dealings would not go on without the knowledge of the local ruler, who would receive his due portion from this man: moreover he would realise the value to him of one who knew of the movements of these Nomadic Fulani. On the other hand, it was safer for the Nomadic Fulani to have some connection with the rulers: for one thing, it would be known where there was any large body of cattle, and, without some such connection, the owners would be liable to attack from any quarter, so that, staunch fighters as they were, it would be advisable to be free at least from the cattle-raiding parties of the ruler in whose country they grazed their cattle, and an intermediary with the ear of the ruler would be an asset.

Thus the scholar would in many cases become the go-between in the ruler's dealings with his nomadic relatives; and, in course of time, an intermediary between the ruler and the Nomadic Fulani frequenting the province. On entering the province for grazing, the leader of a tribe, or section of a tribe, would inform the ruler, through the intermediary, of his arrival and whereabouts. The nomads would escape the tax on industries and on farms, levied on the Settled Fulani; but seasonal presents of cattle would be made to the ruler, and his goodwill retained. It may be noted that, even now, the truth of an important resident Fulani chief's estimate of the number of his own and his followers' cattle is accepted for tax purposes.

Again, though chiefship among the Fulani is hereditary, it is liable to the choice of the members of the clan present, in that they may reject the eldest son of a deceased chief on account of his character, and elect a younger brother. On account of disputes, and lest trouble should arise later, the election of a chief might be done before the ruler, as witness, and as supporter of the chosen man should disagreement occur subsequently. (Election is confirmed by elder Fulani chiefs, who then give the new chief a few words of advice on leadership.)

It became customary for the town-dwelling intermediary to follow the nomads, who had a connection with the ruler of a certain province in the manner described, into any other province to which they might have migrated, in order to collect from them the tribute 'chofal', paid in cattle. Such was the custom at the time of the British occupation, and it was continued for the next few years in the altered form of cattle-tax.

Cattle were given as 'zakat' (locally zakka) and, even now, some annually take out 'zakat' as a voluntary gift to the local Imam and to the 'modibbo' teacher of young disciples.

The relationship between the chiefs of the nomads in bush and the important sedentary chiefs at the present day is remarked on later.

LEGENDARY ORIGIN

Fulani legends regarding their origin, and the origin of their language and their cattle, vary considerably. As regards their origin, they always speak of it as having been from the East : an Arab connection is spoken of in these legends. As to the origin of their cattle, invariably in my experience, these originated " from a river ": some speak of the Barebari — Kanuri — first having cattle, and of the Fulani acquiring cattle from them. The various legends are well known and some of them are in writing.

One legend of the origin of the language is that a child was born who was not known to be a 'Fulani', since in those days there was no such language : later another child was born to the same mother. One day, not long after the younger child had been born, the mother went out to wash herself. The younger child started to cry during her absence, and while the mother was approaching the home on her return, she heard the elder child comforting the younger in words that she did not understand ; but which were understood by the younger child ; " Jeda, inna ma wartai " (" Be quiet, your mother will come back "). She called another, who also could make nothing of these words. Both children grew up speaking this — Fulani — language ; but they also understood the language of their mother. And this is the origin of the Fulani.

As to the Fulani acquisition of cattle from the Barebari, the same narrator says that it was foretold that certain riches would appear from out of the water : these riches were cattle : the Sirati'en (Barebari) first obtained them : later two Fulani entered among them. These two withdrew to a place some distance away and lighted a fire and (the) cattle rose and went to where the fire was : this is how Fulani obtained cattle.

A legend as to the origin of the Nomadic Fulani is that a woman of the Settled Fulani gave birth to a son. One day she quarrelled with her husband and left him in a temper, taking the child into bush. She put the child down, and after a while returned home, forgetting him. Later on he was missed and, though they went into bush and sought for him, he could not be found. The child grew up in the bush, and had become a youth, when one day a spirit appeared to him and informed him that, as he had lived all his life in the bush, so would he continue to live ; but that he would have riches : the spirit instructed him to go to the river and, when he saw a white cow come out of the water, he was to turn round and walk away from the river, and the cow would follow. The youth did as he was told : he saw the white cow come out of the water, turned round and walked away : he walked away for a long time, but at last turned round to ook, unaware that, all this time, white cattle had been coming out of the river and following him, and that there was now a great number of them. Immediately he turned round they ceased to come out of the water. The last four were red cattle, and this exp ains why white cattle are far greater in numbers than red cattle.

The youth continued to live in bush. He married an Arab girl : they gave birth, and their sons and daughters, who were very light-skinned, married each other. Their cattle increased and increased in numbers. The descendants continued to marry between themselves : they have kept to the bush and do not go to the towns and marry.

This version, given by a man of Jafun descent, appears to be appropriate to the Jafun tribes, which are divided, some being nomadic and others semi-nomadic, but of common origin.

CHARACTER

As to character, a Fulani or 'Pullo' (pl. Fulbe) has an innate sense of what is decorous and proper ; is polite and respectful in manner to his seniors : capable of great fortitude ; of bearing great pain or affliction without showing his feelings : reticent regarding his affairs and, as a rule, his wrongs, real or fancied. He has a deep sense of shame. Unjustly humiliated, he will never forget the wrong done to him — it is said that elders, in some such instances, pine away and literally die of shame. Justly punished for an offence he was wilfully committed, he is usually quick to "forgive and forget". He is of a generally cheerful disposition. On the other hand, bad blood is engendered in "affairs of the heart", which may lead to woundings ; while there are some who will stoop to the meanest tricks in order to revenge themselves on another. Intrigue and jealousy occurs between office-seekers.

As prevaricators and artists in subterfuge, Fulani (Fulbe) would I think, hold their own in any company. As a whole, Fulani are very quick tempered ; very sensitive ; easily take offence ; strongly resent an insult, which they do not take " lying down ": after high words, however, the matter is usually considered over, especially where others intervene as pacifiers.

In affrays in which staves, knives, swords, or other weapons are used, a Fulani will usually give a good account of himself : he is not liable to run away.

Of the superior intelligence of the average Fulani there can be no doubt ; but their character in general would appear to retard their advancement. Their suspicion of strangers, with attendant reticence and evasiveness making even friendly advances difficult ; and their inherited feeling of superiority to those peoples among which they dwell ; has maintained a barrier between themselves and all but a few outside their race.

While the customs and characteristics of the various tribes of Nomadic Fulani (or 'Cow Fulani', 'Bush Fulani', as they are often called) are varied to a considerable degree, one can generalise to some extent.

Some customs are common also to the 'Settled Fulani', and certain remarks must apply to a greater or less extent to these.

In considering Nomadic Fulani as a whole, the type ranges from those who never spend more than a few days in one place ; through those who have no centre to which they return for a season, but continue to wander with their whole family, making more or less prolonged seasonal camps in any locality which suits them ; to those who have a centre where the aged and some of the other members of the family remain, and which is visited from time to time by those members who graze the herds — such as some of the Kano country tribes which spend the rainy season about Bornu, Hadejia and Katagum ; bring their cattle down to the proximity of their 'home town' ; leave some milking cattle and pick up dry cows and other stock, and proceed to the Nassarawa area of Benue Province for the dry season, returning North again with the advent of the rains.

It will be found that the majority of these nomads have a more or less circumscribed circuit of seasonal grazing, unless and until something occurs to cause them to make up their minds to vary it and try their chances elsewhere.

Many remain for several seasons about one area and then forsake it for another at greater or less distance ; possibly returning a few years later if they find the new area less suitable to their stock, or in their estimation in some other way unsuitable : such as some of the members of clans of Katsina — Kano origin, for many years moving about in the Southern areas of Sokoto Province, who went as far as the Bayaro area of Dahomey in the last four years, which excursion had not, I understand, been undertaken before ; but who are now returning.

Major migrations take place over a series of years, a few members — the scouts — leading the way and sending back reports as to conditions, when, if favourable, others follow ; so that, gradually, some thousands of cattle belonging to many families are moved to a distance, the time elapsing before the movement is completed being numbered in years. Of this type is the movement off the Jos-Pankshin Plateau, commencing in 1932, and reaching the Chamba area of Southern Adamawa and Muri in 1933-35, whence many Fulani passed East to the Cameroon Highlands. This gradual movement — they may spend some seasons *en route* — was still in progress when I visited Southern Adamawa in 1937 and met Fulani whom I had known about Pankshin in 1930.

I am told, however, that the movement onward into French Territory to the East received a check when the authorities there prevented some of the Fulani, who wished to return, from bringing their cattle with them, so that those following did not go forward as they had intended.

Mention of the Kano-Katsina Fulani above, as being in the Southern part of Sokoto Province, recalls to mind another big migration, of Fulani from Daura, the elders of which say came about on account of a desire for new grazing grounds. This movement was gradual, *via* Zungeru area, thence to Kontagora area, whence some pushed on to Yauri Emirate and the Southern part of Gwandu Emirate, and more to the hill areas of Rijau and Zuru, which they reached about 1907-1908. They are present in these areas in large numbers, with big herds of cattle, which they say have increased considerably in numbers during this period. Their important chiefs came with them and remained in central positions : their descendants now retain these chiefships.

As in past times, the movements appear to be due to two main reasons : a search for new pastures and an unexpressed, but nevertheless keen, desire for independence and freedom from what they consider unwelcome interference and supervision by authority.

Following the British occupation of Kano and Sokoto in 1901, there were considerable migrations of Nomadic Fulani, and many have never returned : these migrations appear to have included many Wodabe.

The first great reason for these movements, the never-ending search for new pastures, includes a strong desire to keep their cattle away from those of the Settled Fulani, which they accuse of bringing and spreading cattle diseases wherever they go, and which, in these days, are for ever invading areas hitherto almost the preserve of the Nomadic tribes.

Regarding this distrust of the cattle of the Settled Fulani, the Nomadic tribes, wherever that may be, keep their cattle well apart from those of local Fulani. On each occasion on which I have visited the Chamba area of Southern Adamawa, I have been urgently requested by the nomads to supply a separate inoculation ground for them : they kept their cattle separate from those of the settled Adamawa Fulani, which were "full of diseases", and did not wish to mix with them at an inoculation camp. At our camp in Yauri Division of Sokoto they always have the greatest suspicion of the non-nomadic herds which come in, keeping their cattle well apart from those of the Settled Fulani, and virtually reserving one end of the inoculation ground. In both cases they keep the cattle apart during the period of quarantine and on the day of release. I was told recently that a considerable number of Siwalbe who had for some years been in Nassarawa area of Benue Province, to which they came from Kano and Bornu, had returned whence they came owing to the increasing prevalence of Settled Fulani cattle.

Sections of various tribes or clans may be found over an area of thousands of square miles, in many instances sections being so far separated that they have no knowledge of each other, though they acknowledge being of the same tribe. In an area favoured by Nomadic Fulani it is usual to find families of a number of clans (of, for example, Kano Province origin) often lightly interconnected by tie of locality ; such families, or parties of families, keeping their camp, or camps, separate from those of the other clans, though freely mingling socially.

It is interesting to find, on making enquiry, that so many ascribe their origin to so few small places, notably the large numbers who claim origin from places in Katsina and Kano Provinces, for example, Bebeji; Shanono (which the majority of Siwalbe speak of as their place of origin); and the numbers of Jafun origin.

In many cases the connections refer to the comparatively distant past, neither the informant nor his father having even visited the place of origin. It would appear that they often have reference to that time when some early ancestor, perhaps the clan founder — since genealogies are not traced as far back as the clan founder or common ancestor — found a favourable spot about which he grazed his cattle for some period. As the family group (or patrilinear clan) increased and the number of cattle multiplied, the group or clan would split up. Then, as now, the cattle would be divided, and the younger members seek more extensive pasture grounds, thus easing the local pastures and ensuring that they did not become cattle-fouled, and at the same time minimizing the risks of an outbreak of disease.

While the elders might remain as a family centre to which the younger members returned at intervals, gradually the group would split up as those who married, and were given or inherited cattle, became independent and in their turn had offspring. Then, as now, members would from time to time visit their relatives until the death of those nearer related to them, or distance and, in the old days, the dangers of travel, severed the link and created a separate entity.

Nevertheless, there is constant intercourse over vast distances; visitors are constantly coming and going, or emissaries being sent from place to place; while those on a journey avidly exchange news and gossip with acquaintances they meet. The speed with which these Fulani transmit news is proverbial. The whereabouts of any head of a family of Nomadic Fulani, within an area considerably greater than, for instance, Sokoto Province, is usually ascertainable without having to ask more than one or two members of the Nomadic clans.

In the period of misrule by the Fulani overlords during the latter part of the nineteenth century, Nomadic Fulani did not escape cattle-raiding parties sent out by rulers into adjacent countries against which they were warring; but they were less easy to discover than the Settled Fulani, and in many cases the wildness of their cattle militated against the success of the raiders in getting them all home.

At the coming of the British it was found that there was a 'tax' on nomadic cattle, apparently little more than a grazing fee or tribute, or as much as could be obtained in cattle from the owners, since no general rate was imposed and, doubtless, then as now, owners had little to learn in ways of evading payment.

DECIMATION OF HEADS BY DISEASE

Of profound influence on the history of the cattle-owning Fulani are great losses of cattle through disease, chief of which has been Rinderpest. In the years 1887-1891 a great outbreak of Rinderpest decimated the herds of cattle-owners. Starting apparently about

Darfur, the disease reached what is now the French Colonie du Tchad in 1886, spreading straight from East to West. In the greater part of present-day Nigeria the disease wiped out the great majority of cattle. This outbreak was commonly known in Hausa as 'Sannu', from the Hausa greeting used as an expression of sympathy. The older men tell one terrible stories of those days. Attempts were made, by some, to fly from the disease and preserve their cattle. Fulani, having lost all — or nearly all — their cattle, became demented: many are said to have done away with themselves. Some roamed the bush calling imaginary cattle: assaults on persons for imagined provocation or suspected derisive remarks as to loss of cattle were common. When the outbreak had spent itself and passed on, Fulani of the eastern areas of what is now Nigeria renewed their cattle from parts of Adamawa that had escaped, while those to the West obtained the almost humpless 'Keteji' type kept by the Borgu Fulani from time immemorial, hardly cattle of the bush and hills of Borgu, Kaiama and Nikki, which had apparently escaped the ravages of Rinderpest to a considerable extent. So great was the demand for cattle that, locally, it was common in many places to offer large prices for the unborn calf.

In 1913-1914 was a further widespread outbreak causing tremendous losses, following a great drought and famine over a large area : this was known by some as 'Gamagari' (Hausa), from its being general over a wide area.

Again, in 1919-1920, another widespread outbreak devastated Fulani herds ; "So that even hyaena did not eat the bodies of the dead cattle." It was known by some as 'Docchal', because of the few cattle it spared in a herd ; 'docchal' being Fulani for a remainder or remnant.

The disease, of course, took its toll in the years between these great outbreaks, and continued to do so, to greater or less extent, until the introduction of preventive inoculation by the Veterinary Department, which quickly became popular, and within a few years this scourge of the Fulani was under control. The losses in cattle must have been enormous : even now many Fulani say that they have by no means the number of cattle which they used to possess before the latter outbreaks. While some were fortunate and able to keep going the strain of cattle they had inherited, many were reduced to such nonderscript herds as they could build up in the course of time, so long as they consisted of cattle of some sort ; perhaps establishing a type later, as the herd grew. A common explanation for possessing cattle of a type differing from those traditionally possessed by the tribe (for example, a Bodado, whom one would expect to have red cattle, possessing those of 'White Kano' type) is a laconic ; "Soinde na'i" — "Lack of cattle." Following repeated outbreaks, many of the Settled Fulani have never replaced their lost herds.

Of the Nomadic Fulani, it may be said that cattle are his life ; they are "in the blood" : he has no other trade, and he may have no other possession — some do not even keep sheep as a side-line. Without cattle he is lost. Should he be deprived of all his cattle through disease or other misfortune, his one idea is to re-establish a herd. It is a characteristic that in many instances, if they have escaped his misfortune, his relatives and friends will help him with gifts of cattle. Otherwise he must make shift for himself. He will tend a herd for another, who lacks a son or other suitable herdsman, for his keep and for a gratuity of a heifer, preferably, or a young bull, at the end of the season.

He will undertake a spell of labour, more frequently cultivating a farm for a season or two, moving to a village for the purpose : any shift which will mean cattle of his own eventually, and future independence. It is not uncommon to hear of a man restarting a herd literally " ab ovo " — purchasing a hen, setting the eggs, setting the eggs of the progeny ; selling some of the fowls and buying a goat or goats and, eventually, from their increase, being able to purchase a heifer. It is well known that a Fulani will practise great self-denial when the necessity arises.

COMPARISON BETWEEN NOMADIC AND SETTLED FULANI

Some of the differences between Nomadic and Settled Fulani, as seen at the present day, are significant of the gulf that lies between them in social outlook.

The Settled Fulani scorn the Nomadic types for their laxity in their religious outlook, and undoubtedly adhere far more strictly to the tenets of Islam : whereas they keep their wives in seclusion — the modified purdah of the common people of these areas — the Nomadic tribes have no purdah. The Settled Fulani has his marriage legalised according to Muhammadan law. The nomads have a procedure which entirely dispenses with any legal form, and there is a system of informal divorce and remarriage with no period of ' iddat ' before a woman may be remarried. (Frequently a married woman will meet by arrangement another Fulani who will take her to his home and, paying the bride price, marry her without further ceremony.)

The Nomadic tribes say that the Settled Fulani marry without sound order or sense and without selection ; hold them in contempt for marrying non-Fulani, scorning them for tainting the blood.

While the Settled Fulani look on the nomads as ' pagan ', the nomads look on them as ' degenerates '.

They do not seek each other in marriage or, if so, such is still unusual, exceptions being such instances as when, for example, on account of not begetting progeny, a nomad is advised to marry a woman of a tribe of Settled Fulani.

Again, the Settled Fulani may scoff at the Nomadic for living under hard conditions — " too mean to part with a beast in order to live well " — getting little out of life, exposed to all weathers and growing old quickly in looking after their livestock ; while the Nomadic say the Settled Fulani are poverty-stricken, and accuse them of selling their stock in order to satisfy their desires, luxuries in food, fine clothing and the like.

Fulani whose main interest is in cattle-rearing often say that their chief reason for not building themselves better houses, such as clay-built, thatched huts, in place of rough shelters constructed of leafage, grass, cornstalks, bamboo branches, and the like, where circumstances may well permit of such—for instance, where they have a permanent centre—is that this would tend to make them lazy and neglect their cattle, especially at night and early morning.

The great majority of typical Nomadic Fulani do not farm except, as a rule, through poverty of cattle ; or prefer, if cash is available, to hire others to do the work. In saying ; " I have never used a hoe and, God willing, I never shall ", the speaker indicates that it would only be through misfortune and loss of his cattle that the necessity to farm would arise. Further, of course, to one not brought up to it, hoeing, never a light task, is heavy work.

This would not refer to such as a number of the Jafun tribes who farm an area, usually near a 'habe' (*i.e.* non-Fulani) village, store their crops at the village, and then proceed with their cattle to the dry season grazing areas. One would more properly class these sections as semi-nomadic.

It is common to find Nomadic Fulani living in contiguity with pagan tribes : it is convenient to the Fulani to live near pagans, and, in many areas, a pagan hamlet in cattle-grazing country will not be in existence for two years but a Fulani makes his encampment close to it.

From the pagans the Fulani family will obtain food and other commodities at cheap rates : milk can be easily exchanged for corn et cetera, and the Fulani do not, therefore, have to sell a beast from time to time, as would probably be the case in 'Hausa' country, where it would be necessary to have cash available to supplement that realized by the sale of dairy produce, in order to *buy* foods.

At harvest time is the advantage of stubble grazing on the pagans' farms. (In some cases, but relatively few, manuring is valuable to the pagans.) A more subtle reason is that often the guileless, good-natured pagan leads himself into being made useful, even to the extent of bringing together a band of workers to help his "Fulani friend, who is badly off for man-power, to get some little farming done ".

They do not intermarry, neither side desiring the other in marriage.

CULTURE

Literacy is practically non-existent among the Nomadic Fulani : there are few educated persons able to read and write Arabic, much less those learned in Muhammadan doctrine, among them ; nor do they put their sons to the schools. In one large area popular to these Fulani—numbering hundreds—I know of none who is literate among the tribes represented locally, though there are two members of the Ba'en tribe, neither of whom are in the area, who are learned scholars. The lack of learning among them is accounted for, by them, by their being fully occupied with their cattle—as is said ; " A man of property has no time to spare." It would be possible, having lost his cattle, or handed them over to the care of others, for a man to dwell in a town and within a short time become a ' modibbo ' (man of letters), having no other work with which he must occupy himself, and thus applying himself wholeheartedly to scholarship. It is obvious and, indeed, agreed by all, that the nomads are quick learners and intelligent subjects.

The Nomadic Fulani are undoubtedly, as a whole, lax in their attitude to religion. I have read, and heard the statement made, that they are pagans ; but personally I do not know of a camp in which the orthodox Muhammadan devotions are entirely disregarded, while it is usual to find that a number of persons of each camp are in possession of a rosary.

They may be, and in many cases indubitably are, very wayward, frequently breaking the laws of ' haram ' (utterly forbidden). Their marriage customs are commented on elsewhere. Moreover their superstitions, belief in omens, rites and practices proceeding from superstitious belief, are often marked to a degree.

Many of the younger members appear especially lax, and some of the elder never abandon their lax ways ; though others, as they advance in years, pay more attention to religion. It is not uncommon to find, in a younger man at least, when required to take oath upon the Koran, that it is necessary to enquire further as to his knowledge of the set daily devotions for, though he says he does perform them, it is often found that his is only a very superficial knowledge, and he is not fit to take the oath in that manner.

While the strictly orthodox may contemptuously dismiss them as ' pagans ', enquiry would reveal them to be ignorant Muhammadans ; at the lowest, nominal Muhammadans.

There is a ' Fulani code ', ' Pulaku ' (the word has other meanings), which is common to all Fulani, though variously interpreted according to public opinion of the various communities. ' Pulaku ' deals with morals and manners which regulate the conduct of a Fulani in his dealings with others of his race and people of other races ; the proper behaviour as between young people and elders ; customs and principles. While public opinion usually guides the enforcement of this moral code, hearings, decisions, and penalties for breaches, may rest in the hands of elders.

Out of respect for them, Fulani do not use the names of certain relatives when speaking of them. Most usually such include the name of one's husband, the father of one's wife or of one's husband, and the mother of one's wife or husband, sometimes of one's father.

A person with the same name as one's father may be addressed as ; " My father's namesake ", in order to avoid mentioning the name.

The Nomadic Fulani appear to carry the custom further than other types, and may include the seniors of the community ; the friends, being contemporaries, of their father ; the maternal uncle.

Some do not speak the name of the local ruler (common also to the Hausa), nor of their own chief or ' ardo '.

A period of some forty years of peaceful conditions, following the establishment of British administration, has naturally had some effect on the Nomadic Fulani, with changed conditions everywhere about them.

Prior to this era, few of them spent any time in the villages — it was not safe for them to do so, as they might be held to ransom to be paid in cattle by their relatives. Nowadays it is common to find that a considerable proportion of the elders, and others who do not graze the cattle, spend much of the time in nearby villages, returning to the camp at evening. There is today less necessity to guard flocks and herds closely.

There is also a tendency in some quarters to a breakdown of some of the old customs, such as the traditional custom of inheritance giving way to the distribution of the estate according to Muhammadan law ; marriage customs, and the like.

It is regrettable to find, during this period, that at least one instance of the lack of the stricter morals of other days has, in some families, brought retribution. Women visiting the towns to sell dairy produce in past days would scorn to accept the advances of a townsman, whereas in these days some are not averse to acceding, with the result that a number of half-Fulani progeny are born into the families : considerable trouble is now often experienced by the older Fulani, where this has occurred, to get them to take an interest in the cattle : older men deplore the fact that they cannot get youths to remain at the camp ; the recalcitrant youths behave to their elders as no true-born Fulani son would to his parent.

In pagan areas where brewing and fermenting of alcoholic drinks is not restricted, a deal of drinking is indulged in by a number of the men : this is true of some sections which have left the more strictly Muhammadan areas in comparatively recent times, and who used not to drink.

Even so, a laxity in certain directions, and a tendency towards easier living, does not appear to be general, and has hardly affected the customs of large numbers of them : the old customs still hold : residence in, and migration to, the less thickly populated areas among unsophisticated peoples, and age-old traditions that have stood the test of time and varying conditions, would appear to be factors in ensuring their continuance.

DISCIPLINE AND LEADERSHIP

Fulani used to have their own method of dealing with criminal offenders among themselves, such matters being in the hands of a council of elders called together for the purpose. Except in the case of slaves, no imprisonment took place, since it is supposed in the case of Fulani that, if imprisoned, their fortune is dissipated for ever. Nor would the offender be driven away, such being shameful to the particular community to which he belonged. The method was to take some of his livestock. A bull might be taken and slaughtered and the whole community partake of the meat: or stock sold and the proceeds distributed among them. In the case of manslaughter, compensation for the relatives of the dead person (diyya), also, was exacted, and to double, or more than double, the amount of that imposed by a court. Perhaps, from a herd of 100 head of cattle, twenty or thirty head would be taken, some twenty or so for the relatives, and the remainder for the collected elders for their trouble, especially onerous in such cases, in persuading the injured parties to forgive, and avoiding what might well become a 'blood-feud'.

It is thought that these Fulani 'courts' persisted up to some twenty years ago.

Where a young man takes to extravagant ways, enjoying the pleasures of the towns, fine clothes and the like, to the extent that he makes inroads in the herd, cattle being sold to raise cash, he is not infrequently expelled from the home by his father or elders, or, otherwise, leaves home after having been reprimanded, preferring to wander abroad.

As to leadership, naturally the Nomadic Fulani have their own leaders and spokesmen.

Usually the more important chiefs remain about one place, generally in the vicinity of a town, for a number of years, with only a small following of near relations, and a few cattle: they do not move about with the larger numbers of cattle; the members of the clan grazing the herds elsewhere, and not settling by their chief. If he possesses a number of cattle, beyond those kept nearby him, he may see them at the times at which the seasonal grazing brings them into the vicinity, or perhaps not for a few years. Frequently such a chief owns comparatively few cattle.

It is usual to find that a man who has successfully kept together a large herd, and is considered to have good fortune, has a following; having with him his sons and their families; his younger brothers and his nephews, and their children. Such a man may assume or acquire a title, and a title is inherited by a son or brother.

A chief (for example, 'ardo', = leader) has little or no authority beyond his closer relatives. The clan will, of itself, collect round a good 'ardo'—he has not the authority to collect it; but will disperse from an unpopular one.

A successful man, having collected a considerable following, would assume a title in an area other than that wherein the senior chief remains: should he visit the area in which the chief dwells, even though this chief should be poor in cattle, he would still acknowledge him as his superior in chiefship, and profess his own allegiance, and would, if in the vicinity, pay him a courtesy visit. If he had dealings with the local ruler, such would be done through the medium of, or in company with, this resident 'ardo' or chief. Thus, at a given time in a certain area or emirate, some clans will be found to have no chief, while some have more than one. Members of a section of one tribe with no local leader or 'ardo', having become separated by distance from any chief of their own, sometimes attach themselves to some other tribe or section of a tribe, with whom they are or have been in some way associated, such as tie of locality of origin, who have a leader or chief who is in contact with the ruler of the area in which they are grazing, or in an adjacent area.

CONTROL OF HERDS

A typical 'Cow' Fulani knows his cattle individually : while he may not know exactly how many he has, he does know if one is missing, and which individual animal this is, and will avoid no exertions in searching for it until discovered. There are names for an almost infinite number of combinations of hair colours, and by these names the cattle are known : the individual animal is often spoken to by that name and, when a Fulani is moving his cattle, many of the cries, which appear to the uninitiated to be nothing more than vague noises made to the herd, are, in reality, calls to individual animals.

Further, it is to be remarked that these Fulani are able to identify the animal of a neighbour's herd, even though not of the same camp or clan, and, from its characteristics, to name the line on the female side, in that herd, from which it has been bred ; so that, if butchers are seen to be leading a beast to the town, the remark ; "That is from so-and-so's herd", is a commonplace.

The ease with which the majority control their cattle — often none too tame — is often commented on, small boys being quite capable of controlling a considerable herd out to graze.

Sometimes control is so good that, should the herdsman desire to keep the wherebouts of the cattle secret, one may pass close by a herd in bush without hearing a sound or knowing that there is a herd within miles, the cattle having remained quite still, being trained to follow the herdsman, and when he stops, as if to listen for pursuers, to remain together, silent, and also listening for any sound from that direction.

I have watched cattle at a camp walk quietly, one by one, into bush when the owner, not wishing me to inspect them closely, spoke to them in undertones — in the intervals explaining to me how he could not keep the herd together. On another occasion, I have heard the light tapping of a staff on a tree send the cattle helter-skelter to the sleeping-place, at a distance, where they all faced about in the direction of our approach : here they could be inspected at will and remain perfectly quiet, whereas in bush they would have scattered ; some herds being so trained — a device dating from the old days, but still found very convenient on certain occasions.

It is not uncommon to see a whole herd follow the leadership of the herdsman at a quick run. Swimming cattle over broad rivers, the cattle following the herdsman, is a specialised art : where cattle are not used to it, it is hard work getting them to enter the deep water ; for several days the cattle may break back and have to be collected for the morrow's attempt : finally, on occasions, some other known crossing may have to be tried, all attempts having failed : extra precautions, with canoe-men in attendance, are commonly taken.

These 'Cow' Fulani take a pride in their cattle, and take care of them: great is the scorn expressed when tick-ridden animals are seen in another's herd — an obvious sign of lack of attention.

Pack-oxen, whose early training is confined to carrying the picketing-ropes or other light bundles, are commonly used for transport, though donkeys may be used to carry young children and the aged. Some of the larger oxen are a fine sight, carrying the bamboo branches 'kewe' (which constitute the portable shelters of a number of nomads); the household and milking utensils, calabashes, corn-mortars and the like; while it sometimes takes a second look to find some young children perched securely among these articles, almost as young birds in a nest.

A number of — or at the least a few — sheep are more frequently kept than not: they can be disposed of when the smaller needs for ready cash arise, obviating the necessity to sell from the herd. Cattle may be sold at any time; as needs for clothing arise; on occasions of the arrival and entertainment of visitors; for celebrations and other expenses after childbirth, etc.; to meet cattle-tax; or to buy food if this is short on account of the amount of dairy produce for disposal being small. The average Fulani does not trust himself to keep intact any considerable amount of money for any length of time.

Before moving their herds from one area to another, or when on the move, nomads are careful to make extensive enquiries as to the state of the area into which they propose moving, gathering all the news they can, especially as regards cattle diseases or absence of disease, and sending members out well in advance for this purpose.

The same holds good, in my experience, in the case of cattle inoculation camps, when a scout is sent on to enquire regarding all conditions: this scout is probably never known to the Veterinary staff; but even if he is known, it will not be any propaganda by the staff which will decide him whether to recommend his people to bring their cattle or not: they will go on his report of what he has gathered from Fulani and what he has seen with his own eyes. More than once, on noticing a stranger, I have told him to look round his friends' inoculated cattle and see how they have fared; receiving the reply; "I have already done that."

Although, with the freer movement of all types of cattle-owner since the British occupation, avoidance of contagious diseases is less easy (a disgruntled old Fulani once said to me; "I never saw all these different diseases until after the 'white men' came: my cattle were all right until everything was changed by them"), these Fulani are successful, often over a long period of years, in keeping their herds free from them. Their calculations are sometimes upset by the presence of Rinderpest in wild ruminants and pig. I recollect a case of this a few years ago, when a member of the Bagananko'en, with his extensive family, brought a total of some 1,600 head of strong and very wild cattle to our Talata Mafara (Sokoto Province) camp. In conversation with one of the sons, aged about 24 or 25, I found that he had never previously seen Rinderpest in their herds : but that some cattle had recently become infected through contact with bush animals, and the whole party, which had been more or less together, had decided to come in for anti-Rinderpest inoculation at once : happily they lost very few cattle. I know, at the present time, of parties of families with large numbers of cattle — in two cases they number well over a thousand head — in a comparatively small, but somewhat isolated area, which have for many years not experienced Rinderpest, nor have they ever brought their cattle for inoculation. I (and they as well) know of other parties which have within recent years lost up to, and over, 90 per cent of cattle from a natural outbreak of Rinderpest ; yet they appear to prefer to take their chance rather than risk some mortality following inoculation, and bringing their herds out of their isolation into close contact with the herds of other owners.

Some of the older men have a surprising knowledge, extending over a vast area, of details of the reputation of grazing areas both good and bad : and take great care to avoid those where 'hendu' or 'ladde' has been known to cause a mortality, even though it were twenty or more years ago : since 'hendu' would include such spore-forming diseases as Anthrax, their attitude would appear to be well-founded.

It would seem that, following the death of such older men, knowledge of this kind is allowed, in some cases, to die with them, or cautions are ignored by their successors. As a case in point, some condition of, or at the time of, the 'black-waters' of the mid-December — mid-March Niger floods, is known to have seriously affected herds, and caused a great mortality in certain years, though not recently : the people who have grazed in these areas in the southern part of Sokoto Province for years, withdraw their cattle from about the river until these floods are passed : but some nomads who have recently arrived in the area are apparently unaware of this state of things (their elders having died, they moved away from an adjacent area where they had grazed for some years), or have not heeded warnings : locally there is much shaking of heads over their folly, for it is not doubted that a mortality will recur sooner or later.

It sometimes occurs that young men — this applies more to non-nomads — sent off for the dry season grazing grounds, discover an area of good grass which others appear to have missed, although adjacent areas are full of cattle ; and only discover some time later, through the appearance of, for instance, Trypanosomiasis, that there was very good reason for the area being left ungrazed.

The waters of various streams and pools are very generally considered responsible for a subsequent outbreak of 'Sammore', which term includes Trypanosomiasis ; and are referred to, by some, as 'ndiyam kewe', that is, the water by which the bamboo Oxytenanthera abyssinica abounds—where tsetse are probably present--which water is said by them to affect humans as well.

Cattle are considered to be ‘ salted ’ to Trypanosomiasis in the course of two years. However, heavy losses from this disease may occur in herds in certain years, notably following a hard dry season which has left cattle thin and weak. I have noticed that some owners spend a season away from a known tsetse-infected area before coming in for anti-Rinderpest inoculation ; return to their ‘ fly ’ area for two or three seasons, and then repeat the procedure ; which indicates that they realise that trypanosome infected cattle have little reserve of resistance against an added strain.

In following a policy of isolation from contagious diseases, it has been the custom to break up herds and avoid having " all one's eggs in one basket " by herding groups of cattle separately on different pasturages. For similar reasons it was, and is, not usual to bring all Rinderpest-susceptible cattle for inoculation at one time, though in some cases even the Nomadic Fulani now do this—apart from young calves ; but still with some trepidation lest some untoward happening arise.

Apart from this precaution, the various sections of Nomadic clans do not make encampments close to each other. They do not buy in cattle, except from a kinsman who may wish to realise for cash in order to buy clothing, salt, etc., and then only a beast which they know through having spent the season together with the owner. An exception is importation of bulls from owners of certain types of cattle renowned for their good qualities, as the ‘ Jabtoji ’ type among the red longhorns ; or some similar particular circumstance ; but never from a stranger or in the market : the Settled Fulani often do buy thus, and perhaps purchase beasts which may have been hawked round several markets ; in this way they frequently introduce disease into their herds.

By this system, combined with that of obtaining news of outbreaks of disease, the nomads reckon they are well able to avoid those contagious diseases which are not endemic. In Nigeria, as a whole, their one great fear is an outbreak of Rinderpest, which they cannot, in the main, avoid, since they may inadvertently cross the trail of Rinderpest infected cattle or bush animals, or water their cattle at the same place.

CATTLE HUSBANDRY

Calves are generally considered immune from (or at most suffer a very mild attack of) Rinderpest, if their dams have had the disease until the rain of the wet season following that in which they are born strikes them ; which means that they are immune until they are several months old, as to the majority, since most are dropped during the hot season just prior to the rains (the time of the early tornados), and during the early rains.

According to some—the following was given by an elder of a Rahaji clan—the site of an outbreak of Rinderpest or Contagious Bovine Pleuro-pneumonia is considered clear after two months : the spot where a Pleuro-pneumonia death occurred must be burned over. If during the rains, Rinderpest and Pleuro-pneumonia infected land must not be grazed over for ten days, so that rain may clean it.

Land infected with 'Hendu'—which may include Blackquarter and Anthrax—may not be grazed for two years (though others may do so—some are said to have a charm or preventative against it).

If cattle die at a wet season camp from 'Hendu,' then cattle which are put on the site of that camp the following wet season will die; but a hot season outbreak does not have this ill effect. No doubt ideas on the subject vary considerably.

The majority of nomads, and some others, warn nearby cattle-owners of an infection in their cattle, so that these neighbours may have the opportunity of moving their herds away, and an arrangement as to separate pasturing and watering places is made. Non-nomads confirm this: it is agreed that non-nomads are as likely as not to hide the fact that their cattle are infected, and frequently camp close to, or let the carcass of a dead beast lie near, the camp of another, from sheer maliciousness, so that they shall not be the only losers. I have often heard of such instances. Should a 'stranger' bring cattle infected with disease into a 'preserve' of Nomadic Fulani, he will not, as a rule, be there long before he is set upon and driven out with the blows of a number of angry cattlemen.

Among antidotes for various conditions, those for 'Hendu' or 'Ladde', or whatever term may be used locally for the diseases which suddenly strike down cattle (with Blackwater, etc.), may more properly be left to the section on superstitions. Cures for many minor disorders are made up, usually from concoctions of barks, herbs and the like. Some claim a remedy for Redwater. Many of the individual recipes are kept a secret to the individual or to the family.

Of more practical use is the vaccination against Contagious Bovine Pleuro-pneumonia. A piece of infected lung is left in milk for two or three days until of a sufficient 'sourness'. A small piece is inserted under the skin of the nose of each beast to be treated, a cut being made to receive it, and the piece pressed well in. Some days later the beasts are again caught and fired, an oval being described about the seat of vaccination on the nose. Other lines are made, one on either side of the face, later, in cases where extensive reaction threatens; in order to encircle swellings which spread towards the neck, in an attempt to limit them.

The method is frequently effective; but is crude, and often leads to enormous swelling of the head; extensive suppuration and sloughing; and a number of deaths. Experts are not always available: it is not carried out by all and sundry; some considerable areas possess nobody with the necessary knowledge and ability.

An interesting experiment was carried out some ten years or so ago in Yauri Division: the idea being to obtain for cattle life-immunity against Rinderpest by exposing them to contact with cattle with an infection which had been noticed to be so mild as to cause no mortality in the herd in which it started. A number of Fulani took their cattle, and what appeared to be a satisfactory reaction ensued: however, some four years afterwards, the cattle were exposed to an outbreak of Rinderpest to which many succumbed. The experiment has not been repeated, to my knowledge, nor have I heard of its like elsewhere.

Reduction of fractures is practised, the animal's limb being set in splints and bound.

Castration of bulls is performed usually when they are well grown and two to three years old, or older, by placing the spermatic cords over a pestle used for pounding grain, and beating them with a cloth-beater's mallet, the operation taking some considerable time, and the animal often taking long to recover fully from the effects of the subsequent swelling and possible other injury. With rams, the cord is beaten with the iron rod used for pressing out cotton-seeds. It is not all Fulani who practise castration of rams, but those who do so say that it is preferable to operate on them when young, by opening the scrotum and cutting the cords : to control subsequent bleeding, the scrotum is filled with a decoction of the soaked pods of ' gabdi ' (the tree Acacia arabica), recognized as a styptic.

The powdered bark of the tree ' kahi ' (Khaya senegalensis) is used on sores and wounds, and is said to be a remedy against maggots.

I have watched with interest the treatment of a punctured wound in the belly of a heifer which had been badly torn by horning, the muscular belly-wall having been perforated, and the gut extruded but not pierced. A rag was allowed to smoulder while the beast was carefully thrown, the exposed gut was returned to place, the prepared rag placed over the gash in the belly-wall and then smeared with hot butter to prevent pus forming : it was explained that if raw butter were used, or if none were available, a handful of grains of corn would be poured in to have the same effect. The flaps of skin were secured by making holes with an awl near the edges, and the flaps sewn together with fibre.

The heifer made a quick recovery. It was obvious that this was not the first case which the operator had dealt with.

Bulls are not infrequently introduced from herds of certain clans which are celebrated for the good quality and purity of type of their cattle ; as, for example, the fine red ' Jabtoji ' type with pure white horn.

If an owner's cattle number twenty or over, he should possess his own stock-bull. The service of a bull is allowed free and in neighbourly goodwill to a small owner, except to a man who has as many cattle as warrant the possession of a stock-bull of his own, or has as many cattle as his neighbours, and has refused to acquire one.

In a large herd, however many bulls there be, the younger ones will not be able to serve cows and heifers, for fear of the ' master ' bull, except in stolen cases ; all the adult cattle being herded together.

If thought necessary to rest the stock-bull from overserving, etc., this ' master ' bull is tied up, and the next in size and strength takes his place. Commencing to serve as a three-year-old, a bull is dispensed with at seven years old, having sired three years' crops of calves ; so that he may not mate with his own progeny, the first of which are now coming to service.

Under reasonably good grazing conditions, heifers will take the bull at three years old, and so calve before the age of four : instances of earlier calving, under favourable conditions, are not rare ; but under hard conditions, heifers will not calve until considerably later.

Cows of certain strains in the herd, mainly in cattle of Settled Fulani, under good grazing conditions, will calve regularly each year ; under hard conditions, cows not infrequently go up to two years between calvings, especially among the red longhorn type, which requires extensive range if the cattle are to do well.

Among cattle kept alongside the large rivers and on their islands (for example, the Niger), and in marshes where there is a good supply of lush grass for the greater part of the year, early maturity is obtained : but the cows soon go off, and are finished with when still relatively young, as a rule ; liver-flukes and other parasites taking their toll. Such cattle may spend much of their grazing time standing in water.

Cattle of certain types kept in arid areas, which are frequently watered from wells only, once daily, at about midday, if introduced temporarily into river areas, are still kept to the uplands grazing of dry grasses, but are taken down to water twice daily, at about 11 a.m. and mid-afternoon (zura), the usual times for watering cattle where water is plentiful.

Endeavours are made to adapt cattle to a new environment by cross-breeding. As an example, some Fulani who arrived on the Niger in Yauri Emirate, some thirty years ago, with the upland White Kano (or Yakanaji) type, decided to spend the greater part of the year grazing the marshes, and purchased red bulls of the local breed of the marshland : they have obtained quick maturity, and cattle multiply at a quick rate ; but are, however, of a nondescript type, mainly of broken colours, to which the name ' Gambaraji ' has been given, and are poor milkers. Other Fulani who arrived with them, and have retained the ' Yakanaji ' type fairly pure, spend less time in the marshes, withdrawing at the early rains, and have the better type of cattle, and better milkers ; but do not get the quick increase.

Another small party which I noticed a few years ago were ' adapting ' their cattle to conditions on the Niger, West of Nigeria, in Dahomey ; purchasing red bulls for mating with their ' Yakanaji ' cows : at the same time they were trying to introduce a characteristic of the red longhorn type—that of following the herdsman when on trek, whereas their own cattle have to be urged on from behind. Since most of them are now back within the western borders of Nigeria, they do not appear to have had much success in attaining the former object. I have not been able to observe as to the latter.

Salt-licks, for which certain areas are noted, are valued ; while prepared native salts are extensively used for cattle, chiefly the white natron (kanwa ndaneha). Some types, salts such as ' mangul ' (manda baleha)—given as a lick or in water where no ' kanwa ' is available ; and ' Foga ' (included in the red type, manda mbodeha) ; are given very sparingly, as they are known to be harmful otherwise. Also used is the salt 'Balma' (of the red type, manda mbodeha), if there is no 'kanwa ndtaneha' available. Common bagged salt of European make has been used to a considerable extent. The natrons and salts are used most extensively from before the middle of the rains until harvest time, and, nowadays, after anti-Rinderpest inoculation.

Marking of cattle, when they are calves, is done by making a slit in the ear, by cutting a section out, or by cutting a hole through it with a knife (jelgol) : branding with a hot-iron is used by some (jelgol chumal).

'Firing,' or marking the skin with a hot-iron, is used extensively ; in circles to limit sites of inflammation, swellings, etc., or in lines or patterns as a remedy against various conditions, such as Streptothricosis.

Apart from the major cattle diseases, a large number of minor sicknesses are recognised, and remedies applied : the names of these sicknesses vary somewhat according to district or tribe.

De-ticking is recognized as a very necessary measure : a precaution against tick-borne diseases.

Where a herdsman is employed, he is provided with clothing and sandals, food and drink : having completed twelve months grazing, he is entitled to a one-year-old bull for grazing up to thirty head (an owner who is well pleased might give a two-year-old) : a one-year-old heifer for herding from thirty to sixty head : if he is able to look after up to 100 head without their proving too much for him, a three-year-old heifer.

Grazing of the cattle may be undertaken in rotation, over a period of seven days, by Settled Fulani, when herds of, say, three small owners may be united and grazed by one herdsman, enabling the others to engage in other work, such as cultivation.

Calves do not go out with the herd ; but spend the day in the vicinity of the camp. By the bigger owners they are not considered as part of the herd until old enough to go out grazing with the older cattle, since they are, as yet, too young to be reckoned as being of any practical value.

The cattle resting-place is situated West of the shelters or huts, the doorways to which normally face West. But if a farm is to be manured round about the camp or dwelling-place, the cattle are moved round at intervals to accomplish this.

Cattle-fouled areas are avoided when selecting a site for a camp, except that land under cultivation may carry cattle year after year for a period sufficient to manure it, when subsequent cultivation again freshens the area for cattle.

A smudge-fire is lighted for the returning cattle, in the evening, at their resting-place — the 'hoggo' or 'walde', the twigs of the shrub Guiera senegalensis (geloki) being used as a rule for this purpose, mainly to drive off and keep away flies, which otherwise torment the cattle (though it is said that certain other twigs have other virtues when burned). A fire is very usually kept up all night, partly as a protection against wild beasts, for which a watch is kept — at least with half an eye.

At morning and evening, each calf is allowed to suck a little from its dam, after which the calf is tied to the tethering rope and the dam milked : having ' let down ' her milk for the calf, the milking is now easier, but if she is a ' difficult milker ' the calf may be tied close to her, or to her foreleg. After milking, the calf is allowed to suck again, thus obtaining the richest milk, until the dam is milked out.

Nomadic Fulani, particularly, like to see a calf in good condition and getting sufficient milk ; but it is said that a good state of health in the dam is of more importance than the obtaining of a great quantity of milk by the progeny, in the rearing of a good calf.

To stop calves sucking the dams when they get opportunity during the day, which may happen in some herds, urine or dung is sometimes rubbed onto the cows' teats, but is washed off before milking time. A muzzle with projecting long thorns is put on a calf to prevent the dam allowing it to suck her when the calf has reached the weaning stage and the cow has not dried off : naturally many calves are weaned through the cow drying off. Sometimes a calf is allowed to continue to suck until it is so large as to have to kneel in order to do so.

When a young calf dies, bran is given to the dam, as an inducement, so that she may continue to be hand-milked : if she is intractable, some Fulani flay the dead calf and dry the skin, which is put near the cow — so that she may smell it — when it is desired to milk her.

ECONOMIC PRODUCTS — DAIRYING

Among the Nomadic Fulani, the women do the milking ; but among many sections of the Settled Fulani, the men do all the milking — for example, in ' Barno Nguddiri ' (Hadejia, Katagum, Misau and Jama'ari).

The dairy work is in the hands of the women : they sour the milk, prepare milk and butter for market, and take these products to the town or village, sometimes from a considerable distance.

After milking, the milk is set aside for souring, which occurs naturally in hot weather, but in cool weather is assisted by first swilling the calabashes used for the souring process with a little of the previous day's sour butter-milk (njonkadam or pendidam) put by for the purpose (often then called njuggam). This sours it quickly — otherwise, except in hot weather, milk may not sour satisfactorily until after twenty-four hours. Certain plants may be used to sour milk, for example, ' dalli ' (Phoenix Reclinata ?).

When curdled, the milk is known as ' danidam ' or 'nyallunde'. This ' danidam,' the cream not having been removed, may be used for whisking and mixing with other foods (it is then known as mburwadam — from the verb wurwa, to whisk), or it may be kept to churn ; a specially prepared large gourd, with a small calabash cap or cover, being the usual churn, which is rocked to and fro on the ground.

It is a common practice, where undiscerning buyers of milk may be imposed upon, to remove cream (for butter production) before the milk is fully curdled ; after which another layer of cream will form, which is left on the milk, giving it the appearance of whole-cream milk, and which the undiscriminating purchaser may think composes the normal consistency of whole sour milk ; the Fulani thus getting the benefit of the extra cream for butter production by selling the milk with hardly any cream in it.

Butter may be made by churning the whole of the sour milk (danidam), as above, or by churning cream removed from the 'danidam'.

From Kano, Katsina, Zaria and to the eastward, the whole milk (danidam) is churned. When churning is completed, the butter is taken out, leaving sour butter-milk — known as 'njonkadam', which is turned out into a calabash : some then add a quantity of water before taking it to market, in order to make more of it.

The butter is formed into balls and put into some of this milk, in which it floats, to keep it from softening or melting, and taken for sale.

In Sokoto Province, down to the Niger River, people will not buy this sour butter-milk (njonkadam) as they mistrust that water has been added to it before sale.

A form of fraud practised when butter is made in the above manner (that is, from whole sour milk) is to continue to churn, after the butter has 'broken' or formed, until the grains of butter collect into loosely knit clusters or lumps, which are then made up into loose balls — the lumps do not coalesce — and immersed in the butter-milk, some of which the balls take up and, when they have remained for some time in the milk, they have the appearance of being solid butter, but actually contain a quantity of butter-milk. This, known as 'belbel', is a white butter.

Such fraud appears to be fairly successful when selling to those who do not know on sight what good butter should be ; but the seller's reputation is likely to become known and, if the market is full of butter, she will have but a slow sale until the supply of good butter is exhausted. An excuse made is that ; "The youngsters overchurned it."

In Sokoto Province where, as has been mentioned, there is no sale for sour butter-milk, it is the custom to make butter from cream taken off the soured milk 'danidam', which cream may then be churned or shaken in a bottle-gourd, or beaten up with a whisk in a calabash, either daily or, where there are few milking-cows, every second or third day, when the product of two or three days' milk is mixed.

The skimmed sour milk (gulutche) is whisked and drunk with foods (being somewhat like the sour butter-milk 'njonkadam' which it has been noted the people of the area will not buy for fear it has been watered).

Unknown to the many, a form of fraud is practised on them by adding water to this 'gulutche'. A little of the 'gulutche' is taken and whisked, and a considerable quantity of water added to it, when it is again whisked to an even consistency. The remainder of the good 'gulutche' is divided into two portions, one part being put in the bottom of the marketing calabash, the treated (watered) portion following, and then the other part of the good ' gulutche ' put on top. Before arrival at the market, it has become well mixed and, should a purchaser remark on the fact that it has become thin or watery, the Fulani explains that it is owing to the distance she has had to walk.

A fraud practised with the butter made in the above manner is, after churning and taking out the good butter produced, to take enough to form a pat or ball, flatten it out and place some sour milk ' danidam ' in the centre, and fold it so that the sour milk forms a core to the ball (which may then be put in milk contained in a spoon or small calabash, in which it is rolled with a rotary movement to remove any excessive marks of tampering) : and so on until all the pats are filled. This is a butter of a good yellow appearance which, after washing and clarifying by the purchaser, become very reduced in quantity.

Butter made from cream alone is not taken to market in the butter-milk ; but, in hot weather only, in order to keep it firm, is placed in a calabash floated in a larger one containing milk for sale or water.

Butter made from cream collected over a period of two or three days, where butter production is on a small scale ; or that made daily and brought in only on a market-day, owing to distance ; may have a sour or rancid taste, or smell, depending on the amount of milk remaining in it ; but since it is clarified by the purchaser as a rule, it is readily bought.

Good fresh butter of a rich yellow colour may be bought, and needs only washing, and salting to taste, to be very palatable for the table of Europeans.

It appears to be an exception for the Nomadic Fulani to adulterate butter.

Other forms of adulteration of sour butter-milk (njonkadam or pendidam) include such as increasing the viscosity and acidity, and thus allowing of the addition of water, by the use of the pulp from the fruits of the baobab (njulandi) or the root of Vitis pallida (gubuwol).

The former method is used where milk is scarce in an area and the people have no choice but to buy what is on offer, and if accusation of such adulteration is made, it is admitted by the sellers ; " So as to make the milk go further. " The latter method is used in order to give the sour butter-milk the appearance and consistency of whole-cream sour milk (mburwadam), with full intent to deceive purchasers : it will go bad overnight. There are other modes of adulterating butter.

It used to be the general custom to wash butter as part of its preparation for market : nowadays, while some wash it before making it up into pats or balls, a great many more do not.

While the majority of Fulani make butter from well soured milk, many of the Nomadic Fulani make it from milk which has not completely soured ; the churning of such milk producing a large proportion of butter of good quality, though rather lacking in flavour ; but yielding a high percentage of butter-fat when melted and all water has been evaporated.

When on the move, and there is no time for further preparation, nomads put the fresh milk into stoppered bottle-gourds and place these among the loads of the pack-oxen where, being shaken by the movements of the animals, on arrival at their destination the butter will have 'broken'; but the butter-milk, only half soured, is not palatable.

Where cash is obtained for the dairy products, it belongs to the woman; the cattle-owner has no title to it. Cash from the sales is expended in buying food for the household, chiefly corn (as noted, dairy products are often bartered for farm produce): in the purchase of clothes for the woman herself: in clothing for the young children including some of the younger herding boys. If the woman sees her way to so doing, she may also clothe some of the older herding boys. Other expenditure is incurred on festive occasions or social gatherings. It is rarely used to help the cattle-owner out in cattle-tax payment, though this might be done as an act of grace by a wife who has had (several) children by her husband. Otherwise, on a later occasion of a tiff, a woman may make it a cause of scornful reproach that her husband could not of himself pay the tax in full.

More probably, the husband will have to pay the tax on any cattle which may be owned by his wife. The husband does not know the amount of money obtained by his wife, the amounts expended, or the amount she may put by. When dairy produce is short, he may have to sell from the herd in order to tide over the period.

By custom, a husband informs his wife when he intends to sell or buy stock, obtaining her views. To be morally valid, such sale or purchase should have her approval.

Most Settled Fulani women and girls are able to, and do, spin and prepare the cotton thread for weaving, to the benefit of their household economy.

It used to be a general custom, still largely followed in 'East Hausa', though I have not seen it in the Western Emirates, of non-Fulani (habe) women to have stalls in the villages from which they retailed the milk 'danidam' (but not the butter-milk 'njonkadam' or the butter).

This 'danidam' was brought in by Fulani girls and young women; when the produce had been sold, the cash and the calabash of each individual was handed back to her to take home. At the end of a week, the older women would come in and give the milk-dealer a present for her services.

Otherwise the Fulani women and girls retail the produce themselves.

SEASONAL GRAZING

When cattle were on the move at about harvest time in the more or less trackless areas of bush, it was usual to break off branches at intervals and leave them lying in the track, or knot together the heads of taller grasses, to indicate the line of trek taken by the cattle, so that those who had been in the town might easily follow to the new camping ground.

Soon after the commencement of the rains, the Fulani leave the dry season grazing grounds and, following the spring of new grass, move towards their wet season quarters, away from the marshlands to the uplands — usually in a northerly direction. They will endeavour to reach the selected area before the advent of cattle-tax on July 1st, though many will not have settled down by that time.

At the wet season camp (dumirde), a zareba or kraal of tree branches, within which the cattle spend the night, is constructed, with an extension at one — the East — end where the herdsmen or owners and families shelter, with a bar-way between it and the cattle enlcosure; and a further bar-way at the far end of the zareba through which the cattle pass to and from grazing. It is not usual for the Nomadic Fulani to make zarebas at other seasons of the year. Some Settled Fulani put the cattle in a zareba throughout the hot season. Some types such as the 'Wodabe' shelter at all seasons under the protection of trees, their coverings for themselves and loads being skins; shelters of other types being dispensed with. While the menfolk construct the wet season camps, the women usually set up the temporary shelters used at other seasons.

Some hobble their cattle two and two at night all the year round: some do not hobble their cattle. The hobbles are sometimes shown as representing the number of adult cattle for tax counting.

The calves are secured to the calf-tethering line after having had their allowance of milk from the dam.

The wet season camp is not broken until the harvest season after the end of the rains — though this does not mean that bodies of cattle are not moved about for various purposes during the rains. Cattle then go at once into the guinea-corn farms, as soon as the crop is harvested, for the 'stubble-grazing' (nyaile), the dry leafage and smaller shoots of the corn being highly prized by the Fulani: in fact, with each Fulani trying to get in before the other, the farmer has, at times, difficulty in keeping cattle off until the crop is safe.

The cattle are now at the commencement of their move towards the dry season grazing grounds: at this period the movement takes place by slow stages, the object being to take advantage of as much guinea-corn 'stubble-grazing' as possible before passing on. Many Fulani make for areas of extensive farming with this object in view.

The grasses of the upland areas will by now be ripening and drying off, or quite dry, and in many areas will consist to a large extent of tall stems, of great value for many purposes, but of little use to the cattle-owners.

In many areas, grass burning by hunters and others has now commenced. The 'Cow' Fulani do little in the way of burning grasses: should a man arrive in an area of dense grasses more than head high, among which cattle have not previously made tracks and trodden down, he will burn in order that the herd shall not divide up and the cattle get lost. It is not unusual, when spending some time in one place, to burn an area close to the camp in order that the calves — which do not go out grazing with the herd — may have the benefit of nibbling at the resultant light crop of fresh young grass that springs up.

By the time that the hot season of the year has arrived, most owners — this does not include those nomads who are continually on the move — will have chosen their grazing area for that period and will probably remain there until after the first rains — chiefly about lakes, streams and rivers, where grass will be most abundant. The dry season camp (sedirde) is often made, where such a site is available, on a sandbank in or by a river, clean and reasonably free from flies.

At the hottest period, just before the rains commence, grass and water are often very short and, especially if the dry season be very hard and prolonged, some cattle may die, and more may be lost after heavy rain has fallen but the spring of young grass still remains scanty. Many herds are in very lean condition, although, under favoured circumstances, a number of owners appear to be remarkably successful in keeping up the condition of their cattle. The types of grasses found on the heavy lands which are flooded in the wet season yield an early, but rather scanty growth of green herbage in this hottest season, especially where the old grasses have been fired. The practice of some (Settled Fulani) to burn the dry grasses of such areas is attributed by others to muddled thinking, since, as nature's time for it has not yet arrived, though the young grasses do come through, they will not continue to grow, and may even be withered up, and so set back, on account of being brought on before their time: such grass burning originated among those who graze their cattle in river valleys and flats of heavy lands, who burn the areas round about them to obtain this scanty growth.

At the early rains, when flies become a greater nuisance, grass round about the camp, or where the cattle are grazing, is often fired so that it continues to smoulder, being damp or partly green, and give off a smoke which keeps the flies away: at this period, too, cattle have to be moved away from certain marsh areas on account of the prevalence of flies.

When the rains have set in, there is a surplus of grass, and the cattle are considered to be soft in condition, although replete.

In general, the shorter grasses are preferred, most especially the short grasses of hard clay soils and marsh areas.

Following the early rains, cattle feed on the plentiful spring of young grasses (daye) until, when the bulrush-millet is nearly ripe and the ground is full of water, they have gradually gone onto the grass 'garlabal' (Fulani), 'karairayau', 'karan kabau', etc. (Hausa), Andropogon (Arthrolepis), which has been growing fast during this time; and continue on this until the time of guniea-corn harvest. Cattle prefer this grass to the others, which they eat only if 'garlabal' is not available. It is not dried off by weather conditions until the coming of the dry, parching, hot wind at that short inter-seasonal period (sollungo) when the guinea-corn is ripe, just before the approach of the cold dry season. The cattle then go onto the farm stubbles, eating the dry leaves (mbafu) of the guinea-corn, the remains of bean haulm and the like, with what 'morsollo' (F), 'harkiya' (H), Digitaria debilis; 'saraji' (F), 'burburwa' or 'furei' (H.), Eragrotis tremula; 'bulude' (F), 'kamsuwa'

(H.), Pennisetum pedicellatum and P. setosum, remain on the farms. Later, when the abundance of farm stubble is reduced, the smaller stalks and the softer parts of the larger guinea-corn stalks themselves will be eaten. The peiod spent on the farms is prolonged as long as it is useful, when cattle then go into bush and eat any type of the dried grass which is palatable to them : the now dry but soft ' garlabal ', and ' chelbi ' (F.), ' datsi ' (H.), Aristida Sieberiana ; ' bulude ' from under bushes : until, at the hot season or ' tornado season ' just preceding the rains, half their food may consist of the leaves of trees and shrubs. After some six weeks of this dry grazing, the hot season will have brought forth a light covering of young fresh grass (daye) in flats and hollows, when cattle will cease to eat the dry grasses, and eat only green leafage in addition to the succulent ' daye '.

In pans of heavy soil where rainwater first lies, when situated about ponds and lakes, a good growth of short grasses comes on before the grass ' chelbi ' does : in similar pans in uplands and hill country, ' chelbi ' only is found.

During the period of the hot season, cattle are also grazed at night where grazing is very short. In certain parts, for example, in Sokoto country, it is the custom of many, from the time of harvest until the early rains, to take the cattle out early in the morning to graze, and return with them to the camp at about 9 to 10 a.m., where they remain for a time, and then go out again until night : others practise this only if grazing is very scanty.

In the rains, the cattle are not let out to graze until the dew has dried off ; neglect of this precaution leading to losses in cattle at the time of harvest. After a night of rain, when no dew can have risen, the herd is allowed to graze in the early morning ; but if there has been no rain, when there will be dew, the cattle will be kept in the kraal until the dew goes off (the cows being milked meanwhile).

A number of deaths during the early rains are said to be due to the fact that, when rains have fallen, the cattle will not eat dried-up grasses, but follow the spikes of new grass, with which, the spikes being short, they take in a considerable quantity of earth.

Some say that feeding cattle on the leafage of lopped branches towards the end of the dry season, though then putting the cattle into good condition, leads to the occurrence of deaths among them in the height of the wet season, and that it is preferable to seek the best grazing available and let the cattle make the most of the dry grasses then obtainable, even though this does entail some loss in condition.

Actually the grass Digitaria debilis is considered the best grass for all types of livestock ; but it is chiefly to be found on farms. Next in value are Pennisetum pedicellatum and Pennisetum setosum ; Eragrostis tremula ; then Thelepogon elegans, known by many of the Fulani by its Kanuri name of ' kagarakagumji ' (Hausa, datanniya).

' Burugu ' (H.), (Panicum stagninum) is found as a river-grass by such rivers as the Niger, about swamps, and in swampy streams ; but is not general : it provides good fodder over a great part of the year for those cattle which are grazed about such areas.

While the above-mentioned grasses are general to many parts, there are, naturally, other areas to which, owing to variation in the flora, the remarks cannot apply.

Very tall grasses are of no use to the cattle-man ; the tops of the shorter, sweeter grasses, and the seeds in the heads — recognised by the Fulani as good nourishment — being greatly preferred by the cattle.

When grazing is so scanty that leaves of trees are considered necessary to supplement the feed, branches of certain trees are cut off for the cattle to browse.

These include ' leggel bali ', which ruminants will readily eat at any time of the year, and is considered the best. Smaller specimens are continually eaten down by wild, as well as domestic, ruminants. Others include ' kawohi ' (F.), ' kawo ' (H.), Afzelia africana ; ' ibbi ', Ficus gnaphalocarpa ; ' shannehi ', Ficus kawuri ; the less general ' shanganehi ', Ficus iteophylla ; ' golombi ', Stereospermum Kunthianum — varying with the trees, useful for this purpose, found in the locality.

In places, the pods of ' barkehi ' (the Hausa kalgo), (Bauhinia reticulata) are pounded and given — sometimes with bran and a little powdered natron — to some of the older catle to tide them over a period of shortage, lest they get so weak as to be unable to get up, or stand, through lack of food.

The fact that little grass burning is done by Fulani has been mentioned.

Grass burning is started soon after the end of the rains by bowmen seeking game, then by hunters with dogs driving game : large areas are burnt in this manner. Later, farmers, in setting fire to scrub in order to get ahead with breaking up more land, may lose control, and then fire get out of hand, as may also happen in the case of honey seekers when smoking the bees for wild honey in the hollow of a tree, or when the dry wood is left smouldering and the tree finally falls among the grasses.

Especially where authorities have given instructions that grass burning is an offence, it is a favourite trick of irresponsible persons to throw a piece of smouldering dung among dry grasses some distance off a path, so that by the time surrounding grasses have caught alight, following the fire being blown into a flame by any breeze there may happen to be, he may be perhaps three miles away from the scene. A more elaborate plan is to take an old, hollow nut of the dum palm, stuffed with dung pressed in through the opening and plugged with a piece of rag. To this a light is applied, and the nut placed among dry grasses : the dung, ignited by the rag, gives off a great heat while smouldering and the nut, glowing as a tinder for a considerable period, acts as a good delayed-action fuse, often used where regulations against grass burning are rigorously pressed.

CATTLE - TAX

Cattle-tax considerably affects the distribution of cattle during the rains, being collected from July 1st to October 31st in Nigeria. Since such tax is not then being collected in adjacent territories under French rule, a number of cattle from near the borders are usually taken over for some, or all, of this period. In general, apart from such factors as grazing facilities and the absence or presence of cattle diseases, the (Nomadic) owner with no ties of residence will consider what treatment he has met with previously at the hands of the district heads or authorities collecting the tax. A really efficient collection in one year will usually mean that fewer Fulani appear in that area the following season — they will probably consider that they have been harshly treated. Numbers will make for an area where collection is known to be less efficient, or where collaboration with collectors, whereby both parties benefit unless found out, is possible. Fulani, especially influential men known to have a considerable following, may, before they have decided where to spend the wet season, be met by a representative of a district head, with presents of kola nuts and (or) a gown : or one may inform a district head that he has arrived in a certain area of his district and wishes the district head to come out and assess the tax himself.

Among the many devices for total or partial tax evasion, a method of total evasion is to take cattle into the depths of a large area of bush at the early rains, with large supplies. Following rains produce a thick growth which hides all traces of any practicable path, and the group remains unsuspected in the area. A number of owners risk the ravages of Trypanosomiasis (' fly ') by hiding their cattle in thick bush known to have a bad reputation for it, in order to evade tax.

Another device is to hide in difficult country, where ravines and rocks make it almost impassable for horsemen ; or in bush that is rarely, if ever, traversed even by the local people, who may, indeed, be afraid of entering it : here hunters may at times lead to the discovery of hidden cattle.

To hide in bottle-necked valleys between steep, rocky hills also bears the risk of being observed from above by such as hunters, and a surprise ' raid ' from the neck of the valley leaves no way of escape.

Here it may be observed that Fulani take good care to keep themselves informed as to the whereabouts of cattle-tax collectors maintaining such close touch with them that their future movements are usually known beforehand, and the news spread where it is wanted. Some amusing stories can be told of this. I recollect asking a Fulani acquaintance where the cattle-tax collectors were on that day : he told me : I then asked where they were making for next : he informed me, possibly without thinking ; but he was correct. An Administrative Officer told me of secret plans he had made with the representatives of the Emir whom he had with him, for a check on a number of Fulani, headed by a chief or 'ardo', settled together at a distance, who were suspected of having concealed a large number of their cattle on the occasion of an earlier count. Leaving very early in the morning, the party arrived about daybreak as planned, only to be met, a little short of the Fulani camp, by the ' ardo', who welcomed them ; he explained that they were expected, as he had been told they would be coming along that day ; and invited them to inspect ; " Those few cattle that we do possess ". No doubt such stories could be multiplied, the discomfiture being sometimes on the one side, sometimes on the other. It seems that, as a rule, if worsted, the Fulani take it in good part, exceptions being when they are made to pay a heavy fine as well as the tax due. It is an amusement of the herdsmen to keep the cattle milling round in order to make counting as difficult as possible, the excuse being that they cannot control the cattle when strangers are among them.

Sometimes, when the owners are surprised, the cattle — especially the wild red type — are dispersed into bush, and scatter over a wide area : the owners themselves may then spend days before they can round them all up. It is useful to have one or more big barreners to lead the way, the others bolting after them on a narrow front : a relic of the old days, chiefly done with the red cattle. In other cases, strong cattle, with youths in charge, are sent to hide in bush, the cows and young calves being kept openly at the camp. Some split the herd, pay on one half, and so receive a receipt which can be made to do for the hidden half if discovered. A well known trick is to keep the cattle on the borders of two territories so that, unless collectors unite to defeat them, the Fulani dodge over the border on the approach of cattle-tax collectors from either one of the two areas.

CATTLE MARKINGS AND ENUMERATION

Many of the names by which cattle are identified are a combination of a primary hair colour, or admixtures of hairs ; or markings such as patches, spots, speckles or flecks ; with a secondary feature. Some colourings or markings are likened to those of certain animals or birds, for example, the red-fronted gazelle, the white egret, the francolin.

A third feature may be added, and the breed of the beast also mentioned. The name changes in accordance with grammatical rules of the language, depending on whether the animal is a male or a female.

To the uninitiated it is difficult to identify by name any but the whole-coloured animals, or those known by the primary coat colour or peculiarity of marking ; while, for the finer points, an expert is necessary : there is not universal agreement on the subject.

Examples are : Baleye (fem.) ; baleri (masc.) ; a black. Felle baleye (fem.) ; pelliri baleri (masc.) ; a black with a white star. Wule baleye (fem.) ; buldi baleri (masc.) ; a black with a white blaze.

Fure (fem.) ; purdi (masc.) ; a grey. Fure raneye (fem.) ; purdi ndaneri (masc.) ; a light grey. Fure sodaye (fem.) ; purdi chodari (masc.) ; a grey roan. Felle fure raneye (fem.) ; pelliri purdi ndaneri (masc.) ; a light grey with a white star. Note :— sodaye (fem.) ; chodari (masc.) ; a blue roan.

Amare, or, amare wodeye (fem.) ; a white with red flanks. Amare baleye (fem.) ; a white with black flanks.

Nore (fem.) ; nordi (masc.) ; a red with a white stripe along the back and along the belly. Nore baleye (fem.) ; a black with a white stripe along the back and along the belly. Nore wule baleye (fem.) ; a black with a white stripe along the back and along the belly, and with a white blaze.

Add to this, differentiations for the various twists of the horns that are recognised, and peculiarities of build of certain animals (and the possibility of marks of firing — also differentiated), which may be mentioned, and it will be realised that the system of identification represents a considerable study.

The method of counting — by twenties — is of interest : the hands are held palm upwards, the fingers extended, and, commencing with the right hand, the little finger is bent for ' one ', the next for ' two ', up to ' five ' ; after which the process is repeated with the left hand to take one up to ' ten ': for ' eleven ', the little finger of the right hand is raised ; the others follow in succession ; then the fingers of the left hand in like succession ; so that at ' twenty ' all fingers are once more pointing outwards.

Many Fulani are poor hands at counting above twenty, when they have to restart up to twenty again. Sixty-two would then be represented by " twenty twenty up to three times, and two " : ninety by saying ; " twenty twenty four times, and ten " : while, with anything above 100 or 120, the computation may defy all attempts to obtain a definite result.

MARRIAGE CUSTOMS AND INHERITANCE

The Nomadic Fulani are endogamous, marrying within the tribe or group. Property is thus retained in the family, and the solidarity of the patrilinear clan is maintained.

The type of marriage most favoured by all Fulani is that of first cousins : among the nomads generally, the marriage of a youth with his father's brother's daughter, and of a youth with his father's sister's daughter, are favoured in that order : while the marriage of a youth to his mother's sister's daughter is not considered good, it is sometimes arranged.

The child (either male or female) of such marriages as the first two is often known among the Nomadic Fulani as Tumbido, a name indicating that it is born of the closest relationship of the line : or, among the Settled Fulani, as Bandado (Bande for short) if a male, and Tumba if female.

Marriages which tend to break down the solidarity of the tribe or group are not favoured. Naturally exceptions occur. As has been said, marriages between Nomadic Fulani and Settled Fulani are rare, an exception being where an older (and wealthy) Nomadic Fulani remains childless with wives of his tribe and is advised to marry a woman of another tribe, who may be of the Settled Fulani if her relatives are willing.

Certain tribes of Nomadic Fulani intermarry, members having taken part in the game or test of ' soro ' (which will be noted later) ; such tribes having past or present associations, probably ties of locality of origin.

Among the Fulani tribes which have for long dwelt in close contact with the Kanuri, the Fulani not infrequently marry Kanuri women ;

but rarely give a daughter in marriage to a Kanuri man. In those areas it is common to find that each race also speaks the language of the other.

Among Nomadic Fulani one custom (known as koggal) is that in which children are betrothed when very young. The girl may be from seven to ten years old, and the boy from three to ten years older ; for example, the betrothal of the son, aged ten, of an elder brother, and the daughter, aged seven, of a younger brother ; the girl's father simply saying ; " I give so-and-so (the girl) to so-and-so (the boy) until she reaches puberty ", and the boy's father sealing the agreement by handing over a bull (ngari koggal) to the girl's father as a token of espousal, the bull being slaughtered and eaten by the relatives. It is the custom for the boy's parents to send presents yearly at the time of the two big feasts (Id el Fitr and Id el Kabir) ; these include a present of money for making the girl's coiffure, a special present given to the girl at these festivals, and kola-nuts in amounts which increase at each presentation. On market-days the lad will give the girl small presents of two or three kola-nuts and two or three pence. The time of their ' marriage' (bangal) will be some six or seven years after betrothal ; when the girl is fourteen years old, and the lad seventeen years old, if they have been betrothed with the preferred difference of three years between their ages.

If relationship is very cordial, each father takes into his household the child of the other, until, one day in the fulness of time, the father of the boy says, in effect ; " Give me your daughter ; I am going to ' marry ' them ", — to which the father of the daughter acquiesces. Those interested are informed, and collect : the girl is taken to the place of the boy's parents or guardian. The presence of a ' modibbo ' (learned man) to read the Fatiha is not necessary. (It appears that at present times a ' modibbo ' is sent for by members of many of the tribes, as customary in the usual Muhammadan marriage ceremony).

In the case of a grown man with cattle of his own, the number of the ' espousal ' cattle is named by the father or the guardian of the bride-to-be : he may propose, say, four bulls. The bridegroom-to-be, or his representative rather, suggests that half that number is sufficient: after some talk, a compromise of, say, three is made. (One large bull may take the place of, and be counted equal to, two small ones.) These are, or were, slaughtered — it appears that at the present time it is permissible to sell from among them. Cloth also is supplied by the groom-to-be.

The marriage is sealed in the presence of the ' ardo ' or ' maudo wuro ' to whom the bridegroom owes allegiance — and who may not live at that camp — (and some call a 'modibbo' from a nearby town if there is none in the tribe section).

To return to the boy and girl who have been betrothed since childhood. The girl having been taken to the place of the boy's parents or guardian, the young married couple then live in a shelter of their own in the camp, the husband eating with his elder brothers, and the wife with her husband's younger sister — if any — at first, and then with the wives or wife of her husband's elder brother or with her husband's younger sister. Both have their duties : he with the cattle ; she with the usual work of the women.

After the wife has spent some two years (or somewhat over) with, or borne a child to, her husband, the couple are allotted, by the youth's father or the elder brother, with whom they have been living, some (say 6) milking cows which the girl will milk, and which, with their progeny, become the property of her husband. They have now a separate establishment, or set up a home of their own, and no longer rely on their seniors for food, but fend for themselves.

Should there be incompatibility of temperament, or friction, between the bride and the seniors, the period of assistance during which the couple are fed by their seniors may be cut short very considerably, and the milking cows given as early as three months after marriage, when the bride has to make her own arrangements to feed herself and her husband.

A girl who has been betrothed as a child may choose to refuse the lad to whom she has been affianced. Should she not wish to marry him, the man of her choice has to recompense the relatives of the disappointed youth for the bull which they handed over to the girl's father when the original betrothal took place, though in actual practice the relatives of the youth do not accept the compensation, it being considered undignified to do so ; but hand it over to the girl's parents. The husband-to-be will, however, have to give to the girl's parents a larger number of cattle as an ' espousal token '. It may be that this requirement is intended to deter others from seeking the hand of a girl who has already been betrothed ; and (or) because the customary right of a party to the favoured marriages — that is, of first cousins — is violated ; as compensation to the girl's family, by one who has not this right, for taking her out of the family group.

Again, a girl betrothed as a child may refuse to live in her husband's home, leave him before cohabiting, and marry elsewhere : or leave her husband at any time subsequently and, without divorce or ' iddat ' period, marry elsewhere. Thus, in some tribes at least, a woman, whether she has not yet borne a child or whether she has borne one or two children by her husband, may elope with — or be ' stolen ' by — another man. Here the technique is to avoid being overtaken by the husband before reaching the home of the man with whom she has eloped. Should the couple be overtaken, grievous strife will occur, during which the woman may run to her new ' husband's home ', or one or the other may take her by force. The matter may be settled by the chief ; but in these days the chiefs are increasingly shy of accepting the responsibilities, for fear that an aggrieved party may appeal against the decision — as an increasing number do nowadays — and apply to a court of law.

Should the couple reach home unmolested and having avoided any ' unpleasantness ', her former husband will later find out to whom the wife has gone and, if the woman has decided to remain with her new husband, he will compensate the former husband in cattle equivalent to those which were given when the original betrothal took place.

The woman may later choose to return to her first husband, in which case the husband she has left, in many instances, does not ask for the return of the cattle he gave as compensation when she came to him : or she may elope with someone else : this may occur a number of times, she leaving her husband in each case without word or indication, but making as if to go on a normal visit to the town, or elsewhere, in the course of her work : the husband will in due course get to know to whom she has gone, and collect from the new husband cattle in place of those which he gave ; except that, in a number of cases, if she has given birth by him, he will not demand such cattle.

The Nomadic Fulani, as a whole, have taken few slave or ' black ' concubines, and in some tribes they never have been taken—in great contrast to the Settled Fulani procedure, and resultant mixed stock.

Where concubines were kept, the male offspring of such unions were not favoured by the Fulani girls of pure descent : though some accepted them, these would appear to be isolated cases : children of concubines intermarried.

Further, among the Fulani, slaves never inherited a Fulani's wife or property.

As has been mentioned, the Nomadic Fulani do not marry ' black ' (namely, non-Fulani) women.

I do not describe the marriage ceremony of those such as the Settled Fulani, similar in its general lines to the usual Muhammadan ceremony, and calling for no special remarks. One custom, worthy of mention since it appears to be becoming obsolete, having become almost rare within the last ten years or so both among those Settled Fulani and Hausa who commonly practised it, is that regarding the consummation of the marriage, when the fact of the bride being a virgin or otherwise at the time of this, her first, marriage, is established. (Such a custom is mentioned in Deuteronomy, Chapter 22.)

A white cloth is spread on the bed on the night of the consummation : in the morning it is examined for marks of blood and, if such are seen, the cloth is handed round for examination : the fact is celebrated by a feast, and word goes round that the girl has kept her virginity (o yari pulaku mako). If such is not the case, the husband exhibits a calabash, through which a hole has been made, on the house roof, or suspended in some other conspicuous place ; when the girl's family have to endure some derision. The custom is said to have become rare since young girls have been less strictly looked after and are not kept about the house as they were in past times ; they now have far more freedom, and wander about at will, often falling to the temptation offered by those who are strangers to them.

A bridegroom is not present when his bride is brought. Custom as to when he first sleeps with his wife appears to vary considerably. Some sleep with her on the night of her arrival. In other cases the bride spends about a week in the house of her husband with younger girls who have accompanied her, and, when they leave, a little girl remains with her until the time that the husband comes to sleep in his wife's hut. Some do not sleep with her, or even enter her hut, for a period of up to three months. The husband does not go to the bride's hut until late at night, and leaves it again very early in the morning ; nor does he visit her during the day : with some, this may continue for from six to twelve months : during this period, others do not inquire whether the bridegroom is " in the house ".

A woman, when she marries into another tribe, or another section of the tribe, remains of her own tribe or section ; but the children of the marriage follow the tribe or section of the father.

Each wife, where there is more than one, has a separate shelter or hut.

Where relationship by marriage does not include relationship by blood, a man does not talk with his father-in-law and, if communication is desired, it is usually done through an intermediary. Nor does the man eat with his father-in-law, and if he approaches or is within the near vicinity, behaves in a decorous manner : should he happen to be laughing and joking with others, he will desist on the approach of the father-in-law.

Where there is consanguinity, this does not apply, the man talking freely with his father-in-law, and discussing ways and means with him, since it is held that such relationship is not as if it were in-laws only, but is as the relationship of an older and a younger member of the family.

The gift of a heifer to the girl when she is betrothed to a youth, or when she is to be brought to the home of her husband on the ' marriage ' day, is said to possess special great virtue. It may be given by the youth's father or elder brother, or by friends of his father, or even by himself, and is not taken to the girl or her parents, but awaits her arrival at her husband's home.

It is usual, among all types of Fulani, for the woman to return to her parents' home when in her first pregnancy, some three months before the due time, to bear her first child there, and to remain until the child is weaned—a period of two years if a girl, and some three months less if a boy. During this time she is not visited by her husband.

Sometimes the period of the wife's residence at her parents' home, after bearing the child, is reduced to a year, owing to circumstances such as her husband's lack of anyone to look after his requirements. Subsequent children are born at her husband's home ; the wife's grandmother, if alive and able, or else her paternal or maternal aunt, coming to assist her during child-birth.

Prior to her return from her first child-bearing, the husband sends money for a special and highly ornamental style of hairdressing (mordi babdi) for his wife, and cloths. The event of her return is almost like a second wedding. She is accompanied by some of her relatives—but not by her father or mother—and by a number of presents, which are handed to her husband's father to give to her husband (who may have sent presents to her parents at intervals after she has given birth).

The child is brought with her to receive congratulatory remarks, and for inspection by all its father's relatives: from this time it will no longer be breast-fed.

With the wife will be brought the cattle given to her by her father, perhaps up to ten or twenty, or so, if he has a big herd; or whatever number can be spared. At the same time the husband is given cattle by his father, or by his elder brother if the father is dead (the elder brother having inherited the cattle).

The elder and younger brothers of the wife—that is, the child's maternal uncles (kawirabe)—if they have cattle, each present the child with a cow (or if they have no cattle, with a sheep), such animals being said to bring good fortune.

Relative to the gift of cattle to the wife by her father, it may here be noted that, under the Nomadic Fulani custom of inheritance, a woman does not inherit cattle when her father dies, and it is by this gift that she will obtain cattle that are to become her own. Before she is married, however, when she has no cattle, she will not be denied a bull, from the herd of a brother, on special occasions.

The child may be taken back to the home of the mother's parents if the father's parents agree, but it is usually kept at their home or, if the father's parents are no longer alive, at the home of his elder brother or, if none, at the home of a friend of about the same age as the young father, or of a younger brother if he already has a wife.

By custom, the father and mother do not call the first child by its name: the reason is said to be that they are, as a young couple, bashful about the child, the father still being almost a lad, and the girl so young, that it were almost as if they were not old enough to have had a child, and yet have produced one. For the same reason the mother will leave the child at home when she has to go to market to retail dairy produce, etc.

If the child is kept by the father's parents (or by his elder brother), they will probably keep him (or her) until betrothed, or until grown up and married, since, if a male, he will eventually inherit some of the cattle through his father. If kept by the wife's parents (or her elder or younger brother), the child will be retained until the age of about seven, and then returned to his parents with a present of anything up to ten head of cattle, or sheep or goats if there are no cattle.

On the occasion of naming a child, on the seventh day after that on which it was born, a ram, provided by the father's relatives, is slaughtered, and the raw meat distributed among the relations: the father's relatives also supply a bull, which is slaughtered for cooking and eating by those assembled. In the case of a first-born it is a custom for the wife's relatives also to kill a ram and a bull for the occasion. On this day the father's tribal marks are incised on the face of the child.

To prevent sickness or evil affecting a child, when two children born before it have died in infancy or early childhood, some leave uncut three tufts of hair, one at each side and one at the middle of the back of the head, which tufts are not cut until the child is about seven years of age. Others leave a strip of hair from the forehead to the back of the head and a strip from one side of the head to the other, forming a cross over the head, similarly uncut.

There is one form of sickness said to be peculiar to Fulani or, at the furthest, to those with Fulani blood in them. It is known by them as ' pabboje ' or ' jonte '. The Hausa refer to it as " The Fulani sickness ". It is distinguished from ' oppere ' pl. ' oppe ' (Hausa zazzabi), feverishness, in that feverish conditions are continuous, whereas ' pabboje ' is typically a headache occuring every other day only, of from four to fourteen days duration : it may be so severe as to prostrate a person for a time. It occurs at the time of harvest.

Among the nomads (and frequently among the Settled Fulani) boys are circumcised in batches of ' age-mates '. They remain in the shade of a tree, near the camp where the ceremony was performed, for a fortnight, their food being taken out to them. After this period, the healing having been completed, a feast is often held, and they then disperse.

In contrast to the distribution of the property (sendugo jaudi) of a deceased person of the Settled Fulani, which follows Muhammadan custom ; under Nomadic Fulani custom, in the event of a cattle-owner dying, his younger brother first or, if there is no younger brother surviving, his eldest son, takes all the cattle for himself, female children of the deceased owner's wives, who are left under the charge of the inheritor, being allotted a cow apiece, which goes with her when she is espoused. Younger brothers of the inheritor, and the male children of the deceased's wives, remain as helpers, but without cattle, until after they themselves marry in course of time.

The wives of the deceased, if they have children, remain with them ; if they have no children, they leave with their cattle, and will probably remarry : an old, childless widow would, however, remain with the family. Following the custom common to most Fulani, a younger brother would take, by inheritance, one (or two) of the deceased's wives to himself. It may here be noted that an elder brother does not take to himself the wife or wives of a deceased younger brother (nor does he acquire his cattle).

It is understood that the administrative authorities are trying to get the Nomadic Fulani into line in the matter of distribution of property left by a deceased person, with the result that at the present day some follow this procedure freely : in other cases interested parties apply to the courts in order to get the customary distribution, already effected, converted into the legal Muhammadan division of the property : in a number of instances one hears of a rapid removal to other parts, by those in possession, in order to avoid the legal and preserve the customary manner of distribution.

On the death of a wife who has lived in harmony with her husband, her parents and relatives will often, if there be one or more still unmarried, give a younger sister of the deceased in marriage to the bereaved husband. This custom holds good among both Nomadic and Settled Fulani.

It is frequently the case that an old man will disperse his cattle among his sons in order that, when he dies, legal distribution of his stock, with the consequent payment of estate duties (ushira), may be avoided. The sons then keep and clothe him and his wife : should he require it, they sell a bull from their herds in order that he may have the means of making presents to visitors and other relatives and friends.

A woman who has never been married is such a rarity that she may be regarded as non-existent among Fulani. It is pointed out, for example, that a very unattractive woman may be the daughter of a man rich in cattle, and that a man poor in cattle will be glad to marry her : or there will be some other circumstance in her favour, however forbidding she may be in appearance or temperament ; though such marriages may not be of long duration.

In the case of a male who remains unmarried, it is most usually on account of his being too idle (being also without wealth) to do more than provide a living for himself ; for example, as a hanger-on to some other person.

Among Nomadic Fulani, following the death of some person in the camp, the place is quickly vacated. Before the elders have buried the deceased, the younger members have already gone off with the cattle.

GAME OF "SORO"

There is one Fulani game closely connected—among many of the Nomadic sections—with the subject of marriage. This game, called 'soro', is said to have originated among the Jafun Fulani, among whom are its keenest exponents ; but is widely practised. It is a test of self-control in which youths of approximately equal strength are matched : in a number of Nomadic Fulani tribes, unless a youth has passed this test, he is not considered worthy of a bride, not having proved his manhood and fortitude. The test takes place before spectators composed largely of those who have recently left off taking part in 'soro', who have much to do with regulating the game ; the unmarried girls, and youths, including those youths who will also take their turn; and others interested. He who is to undergo the test strips to the waist, and wears only an ornamented leather games 'kilt' and ornamental trappings, except that he wears about his middle a stout girdle cut from the hide of an ox, which prevents injury from a blow about the waist. Actually such a blow is foul-play and, except through accident, would only be so placed with intent to injure. With his hands clasped above his head, or holding up some object in front of his face, often a mirror, on which he fixes his eyes as if unconcerned with what is going on, or with the pain felt (that is, out of 'pulaku', fortitude under pain), the 'challenger' stands with legs straddled, prepared to receive without flinching, cuts—usually two—with a specially prepared, strong, supple stick, from the 'tester', a member of a different family, who, after some feinting, deals him a heavy blow on the ribs.

The 'challengers'' part is to receive the blow without movement or wincing, in which they are remarkably successful, very often putting on an expression as if to indicate that they disdain the striker's effort as distinctly poor. They appear to be somewhat assisted by the effects of a concoction of the 'hairy thorn apple' (Datura Metel), which is taken when in course of preparing for the game and produces a strong excitement.

One 'challenger' may undergo several tests during the course of the games, which go on for some three to seven days. On the last day he revenges himself in the return 'match', when he becomes the 'tester' and his late striker is the 'challenger'. Large weals usually result from the test, and these may be visible, as raised ridges, for life: in youth, of course, the possession of a number of weals is highly prized.

The young married men, mentioned above as regulators of the game, will intervene to prevent a 'match' where they consider the conditions unequal, more especially where some of the smaller lads are too daring in coming forward, or in the case of a youth whom they consider is putting himself forward too often as 'challenger'. Should a contestant not agree to another having his 'revenge' on him, they insist that he pays them money—and pays them heavily—to be let off, or else that he expresses humble penitence: needless to say, the former is preferred by the youth concerned.

The game takes place most usually about the time of guinea-corn, harvest (yamnde). The hot season just before the rains is not favoured it being considered that at this period the blood is in poor condition. It may also sometimes take place on the occasion of a marriage; or on the occasion of the naming of a child, especially the first child of a man who has made a great name for himself at 'soro' in his time. It may be held in honour of a chief, as a celebration of his appointment or succeeding to chiefship. Little 'soro' is done at the time of the religious festivals, when dancing, etc., is indulged in. While small parties may commence in a town, the game is carried on, in full swing, in an open space near the town, to the accompaniment of drumming and the shouting of praises of the contestants and of well-known men.

Certain sections of Nomadic Fulani do not intermarry if there is no 'soro' game performed between their members. Some perform 'soro' as a game, but do not intermarry. Not infrequently a girl will get a lad, of a group which does not usually perform 'soro' with her group, to enter the game so that he may become eligible to marry her; otherwise her family will reject him as one without courage and, so, ineligible.

From the foregoing it will be seen that the game is closely connected with marriage custom in many of the tribes (though some sections who perform ' soro ' intermarry with certain sections with whom they do not perform the game).

Among tribes practising the game, a healthy youth not participating in ' soro ' would be shown that he was looked upon with contempt, as cowardly, and he would not be acceptable as a husband to a girl of another family in the tribe, or of another group which performs ' soro ' with his group, and thus conditions would be made generally uncomfortable for him. It would not interfere with the marriage in which a boy and a girl are paired or betrothed when young : the girl, being of the same family, rarely refuses the youth.

GAMES AND FESTIVALS

There are certain other games, or more properly dances, accompanied by singing and drumming ; such as the widely popular ' Fijirde Dampe ', or the ' Gerewol ' dance of the sections of the Wodabe group ; in which one of the objects of a youth in joining in the dance is to secure a wife, since the girls choose those who please them at these dances, which take place at times when a number of tribes or sections of tribes are conveniently close together, so that the members of each may attend in numbers at a suitable centre. A youth will often have fixed on a particular girl, and will make approaches to her after the dance or games at one of these gatherings.

A good deal of sexual licence is tolerated by custom during the festivals of ' Julde Sumaye ' and ' Julde Laiha ' (Id el Fitr and Id el Kabir).

At night, lads give chase to girls, their age-mates, and, if they catch them, intercourse takes place : a number of lads may seize and take their turn with one girl. Young men retire with the girl of their choice—some with the wives of others, young married women who have come from a distance, as have many of the males.

Arising from this, a number of girls return to their homes in-child : if already a wife, the husband accepts the child as if it were his own, but in the case of an unmarried girl having a child in this manner, her affianced may then refuse to marry her, which is the opportunity for another, who would otherwise have had no chance to the girl's hand in marriage, to come forward. If a woman has already borne a child by her husband, he will then, as a rule, refuse to accept an illegitimate child as if it were his own ; and his wife will probably have to get her parents to bring it up.

During these gatherings, besides the games and dancing which take place, there is much fun and jolity ; younger men and youths go from house to house, ' singing ' or chanting more or less meaningless songs, and asking for, and receiving, presents of food from the inmates.

The Fulani share in the Sudanic custom of a ' relationship-in-play ' between certain individuals or individuals of certain tribes.

This allows a freedom to play tricks on one another, between those so connected, which is revived yearly from the tenth day of the month Muharram—the first month of the Muhammadan year—to the end of that month.

The origin of such custom among Fulani is said to exist between cousins the children of the paternal aunt and those of the maternal uncle; but it is general between cousins, the children of a brother and a sister, but not of two brothers or two sisters; between grandparents and grandchildren: between a man and his wife's younger brother, his wife's younger sister's husband, and his elder brother's wife.

The custom also exists between the Fulani and the Barebari (Kanuri) in general, as they are traditionally connected by both races intermarrying with branches of a third race in the distant past, and are therefore considered as being ' cousins '.

The chaffing of each other by playmates of an age is not included in the custom, which allows of practical joking, familiarity and licence of a different order between those connected ' comrades ' having freedom to play tricks on each other without offence being taken, many of which would not be endured by those who are not ' comrades ' in this sense. During Muharram, on seeing such a ' comrade ', one tries to give him a touch with a light switch, or a light slap with the hand, before he can do so; or give chase in order to accomplish this. He must not, by the rules of the custom, retaliate; but may pay a small sum of money in order to escape being so struck. If a ' comrade ' is of such standing that a slap would be out of place, money may be claimed, and he will pay a small sum. If a ' comrade ' is struck and, in annoyance, retaliates, he is jeered at, and it is said of him; " So-and-so has grown a tail." ' Lafolafo ' is the name for this striking of ' comrades ' by one another; ' sidosido ' or ' wannyowannyo ' is the playing of tricks on one another ; under this custom.

DIET

Despite the fact that grain and milk constitute the main articles of the diet of Fulani, there is considerable variety in the foods eaten and in the methods of preparation.

In many cases, herdsmen take a very early morning meal of sustaining character—' ngewari koye ', literally, break fast, and do not take another meal until after they have returned from grazing in the evening.

Some, including older persons, may take a ' snack ' at about 9-10 a.m., the time of day kn own as ' balte '.

The main morning meal, ' kashitari ', or ' mbottari ', is properly taken from about 11 a.m. to about midday; but may be taken at any time after 8 a.m. onwards.

Apart from snacks taken by individuals, the next meal is at night, from about 7 p.m. to 9 p.m. — ' kirtari ', the evening meal.

Foods are :—

Paturi.—for the herdsmen, unable to wait until the daytime meal ' kashitari '. Made only by those with plenty of milk-cattle : peculiarly a meal of the Nomadic Fulani.

Ndinabari.—taken at about 9-10 a.m. by older people, and by others as a breakfast where means permit : it is not taken daily by the whole of the household. It is taken as soon as prepared, and not kept through the day.

Mbordam.—(if milk is in short supply) taken when ' ndinabari ' would be taken, at about 9-10 a.m. What remains over will still be good until evening. It is taken also during the daytime, at intervals, by the young or by the old : for the daytime meal, by such, instead of ' chobbal ' : at night, when some take no other food, nor eat the ' nyiri ' of the evening meal.

Nyamri.—when taken as a staple food it is drunk at about 9-10 a.m. Otherwise it is only occasionally taken, that is, preferred to ' nyiri ' and drunk at night ; and, in Bornu where fresh milk is purchasable, on journeys.

It is taken on the occasion of naming a child, as a custom. The above foods are not made by non-Fulani.

Chobbal.—(Hausa fura) may be taken at the daytime meal ' kashitari ', at or towards noon.

Mbosiri, or Kunuri (the Hausa kunu).—may be taken for the day-time meal ' kashitari '.

Dakkere.—may be taken at the daytime meal ' kashitari '—any time from 8 to 12 a.m. Rarely made by Hausa peoples. Only taken as a change, at rare intervals, by Fulani.

Mokokkorori.—A Fulani food, but also made by the Hausas, of new corn. Would be taken at ' balte ', 9-10 a.m., chiefly only during the time of bulrush-millet harvest.

Nyiri.—(the Hausa tuwo), taken at night, with soup or gravy (li'o) as to the great majority: a few Nomads of the bush take it with milk. While most eat their fill of this as their customary evening food, some will take but a taste of it and (or) prefer ' mbordam ', ' chobbal ' or fresh milk.

The above is not intended as an exhaustive list of foods : various other foods may be taken on occasions, especially when visiting a town on market-day. All types of Fulani are fond of the cakes made of flour of guinea-corn or bulrush-millet cooked in oil or butter (tamsere, the Hausa waina or masa), and those of wheatmeal, or wheatmeal and beanmeal, or beanmeal and guinea-cornflour (cf. H. pinkaso or algaragi).

The preparation of the foods may next be described.

Paturi.—Bulrush-millet is pounded moist and winnowed to separate the bran, dried, and pounded. A little water is put in a cooking-pot and a small quantity of butter put in the water, which is then boiled; the millet flour is put in and stirred — it is not required to be thick like 'mbosiri'.

The 'paturi' is taken up in a spoon and put into a clean calabash, and fresh milk, straight from the milking, put into it; stirred with a spoon; a little melted butter put into the milk, and a 'finger-nail' of salt added. The food is then ready for drinking. Of Nomadic Fulani, and only those with numbers of cattle: it is drunk daily—at morning—to repletion by the herdsmen, who feel no hunger until late afternoon when they return with the cattle from grazing. A wealthy owner may choose to drink it himself some mornings.

Ndinabari.—After removal of the bran, millet is pounded, but the resultant meal is not sifted: it therefore contains coarse meal. Sour milk is mixed in, whole sour milk (danidam, nyallunde, or mburwadam) being preferred to sour butter-milk (pendidam, or njonkadam). Note that 'ndinabari' is *not* cooked.

Mbordam.—After wet-pounding and winnowing of the grain, bulrush-millet is dried, pounded, and well sifted. A considerable quantity of the resultant very fine flour is put in a calabash and some cold water put in, the mixture then being stirred. Other water is put in a pot on the fire until boiled, when it is taken off and, when it has ceased to boil, the water is poured into the flour mixture. When cool it is like a thin, watery 'mbosiri', undercooked as it were, and serves the same purpose as 'mbosiri tainandi' (thin, watery mbosiri) in that it is a drink for children and for the aged. It is taken with sour butter-milk.

Nyamri.—Bulrush-millet is pounded moist, winnowed and washed, and left to dry in a calabash. It is then pounded and sifted, this process being continued until a fine flour has been obtained. A little of the flour is taken and put in a calabash, and a little water is added and worked in with the fingers until the mixture forms into globules.

When this process is finished, the mixture is turned into a steamer (takkirde). A cooking-pot with water in it having been set to boil; upon the water boiling the steamer is placed on the pot, the interstice sealed with moistened bran, and the steamer covered with a calabash or a grass mat.

When well steamed so as to be cooked through, the mixture is turned out. When cool, it is mixed with fresh milk, and drunk: or is taken with clarified butter mixed in, if no fresh milk is available. Only one with a plentiful supply of milk or of butter could undertake to supply this regularly as a meal.

Chobbal.—(for the household: not the steamed coarse meal, with high water-content, made for sale).

After being pounded and repounded until fine, the meal is tightly pressed into balls, which are put gently into boiling water in a cooking-pot, and boiled until cooked, when the balls are taken out and broken up in a mortar, some of the water in which they were cooked being added, and the mass pounded wet, so that moisture is evenly distributed (the inside of the balls was dry-cooked, water not penetrating the fine meal). The thick paste is then turned out of the mortar and pieces broken off from the mass for each person. (That sold in the markets is made up into balls.) Bulrush-millet is preferred, but if this is in short supply 'chobbal' may be made of one half millet and one half guinea-corn, thus getting a taste of the more palatable millet. It is broken up into soured milk and stirred for drinking.

Mbosiri (*kunuri*).—A 'gruel'. After bulrush-millet has been wet-pounded, winnowed, washed and allowed to dry, it is pounded. The meal is divided into two portions. One part is first mixed with a little cold water, and then boiling water, to the amount of about four times the amount of meal, is added: it is then stirred until thick, and left to cool; this is the actual 'mbosiri'. Soured milk is whisked, and the other portion of the meal added to it and mixed well in; a little cold water is added, and the whole well stirred: this portion is known as 'njutari'. When the 'mbosiri' portion is cool, the 'njutari' portion is turned into it. Where no milk is available, the water of steeped tamarind pods, or of the cooked leaves, is used to give flavour, in its place, in the 'njutari' portion. If millet is short, a mixture of half millet and half guinea-corn flour may be used.

Dakkere.—Bulrush-millet is wet-pounded and winnowed to remove the bran, washed, dried, and pounded lightly, not fine. This meal is taken and put into a steamer over boiling water, and sealed up. After a short time, the meal is turned out, and a little boiling water taken and stirred in, care being taken not to make it too moist. It is then put into a mortar and pounded: being then almost of the consistency of 'chobbal', but not so well cooked.

Another method is to pound the millet to a flour, when a little fresh butter is well mixed in: the mixture is then pounded with some water in a mortar; removed from the mortar, and put ready in a calabash. It is said to give condition, increased weight and strength. Note that this is not cooked.

Both types are mixed with whole sour milk or with sour butter-milk, stirred in.

Nyiri.—A porridge taken with soup or gravy. The staple food of most peoples of Northern Nigeria. Coarse meal is put into boiling water in a cooking-pot, the meal being rather less than half the bulk of the water, and boiled until soft, when fine meal is added and the pot covered and left unstirred until this is cooked, by which time the coarse and the fine meal are well coalesced: it is then stirred, and cooking continued for a short time. This is a good 'nyiri' and will last until the second or third day after making.

'Ngajiri', or 'nyiri takkirde', a form made in East Hausa (the Kanuri form). Bulrush-millet is wet-pounded, winnowed, dried, lightly repounded and rewinnowed, left to dry and then ground on a stone, not very finely. A pot of water is put on to boil. The flour is put in a steamer (cf. as for nyamri) and, when steamed, is taken off and all put into the pot of now boiling water, and stirred. Live charcoal is put into an earthenware bowl and this put on the pot as a cover, while the fire under the pot is lessened, to complete the cooking ; the pot being taken off the fire after a short time. This ' ngajiri ' is more pleasant to eat and more friable than the 'nyiri unandi', described above, which is usually made. From Sokoto to Kano, ' nyiri ' is usually made of guinea-corn ; but East of Kano to Bornu, of bulrush-millet : if this is in short supply, it would be made of guinea-corn, to conserve the bulrush-millet for ' chobbal ' and 'mbosiri'.

The above foods may be made of other grains. An undoubted preference is shown by Fulani for preparations made from bulrush-millet, other grain being used when it is scarce.

An ordinary everyday soup for the household is made as follows :—

A quantity of water is put in a pot on the fire and, when boiling, beans are put in, if available : when these are nearly boiled, natron, or a little salt, is added : when the beans are quite cooked, seeds of the baobab (which are made up into cakes) are pounded with red peppers and added. When the mixture has ceased to smell of the baobab seeds, powdered baobab leaf is stirred in—or powdered okra (Hibiscus esculentus) is substituted. The soup is left to boil hard until the smell of the leaves has been driven off and it is well cooked.

Apart from okra ; red sorrel leaves (Hibiscus Sabdariffa), the leaves of Cassia tora, and those of various other plants, may be substituted for baobab leaf ; but at infrequent intervals. The soup, made with baobab leaves, is known as 'li'o bokko': made with okra, as 'li'o kubeje'.

Another kind of soup or gravy, known as ' hako polle ' or ' li'o polle '—from the use of the leaves of red sorrel (the Fulani not making use of the calices as do the Hausa tribes)—is made as follows :—

A quantity of water is put into a pot and the leaves of the pot-herb Gynandropsis pentaphylla, or the ' spinach ' Amaranthus caudatus, and pieces of young pumpkins, Cucurbita Pepo, are put in. When boiled, the leaves of red sorrel are added, and then a little flour stirred in. When again boiled and thickened, a little natron, or salt, is put in. The soup is then ready.

These, as stated, are taken with 'nyiri'.

For people well able to afford it, much richer soups are made, and include meat, butter or groundnut oil or palm oil, several varieties of condiments, with other ingredients. For the purpose of this paper, such soups may be disregarded.

Meat is little eaten, except on some festive occasions, or when a particular urge for it is felt, or ' bush beef ' has been obtained : nor are quantities of meat considered to be of great value in the diet—the " Fulani's meat " is in the milk and butter.

The meat is grilled. When a young bull is killed, the whole of the group is invited to partake of the feast.

Certain other foods used on occasions include :—

Mokokkorori.—Made of new bulrush-millet. A Fulani food, but the Hausas also make it. Good, newly ripened corn, which has not yet dried out, is stripped from the stalk with the husk or chaff and roasted thus, constantly stirred, as it is, on a shallow earthenware bowl. It is put to dry and, when dry, threshed. It is not pounded, but ground until fine (that is, with the bran still on it). The meal thus obtained is steamed in a steamer for a short time, and then taken off. Boiling water is taken and put into the meal, which is then pounded in a mortar (as in making chobbal).

This mixture is drunk with whole sour milk, or with butter-milk if whole sour milk is not available. Though the new corn is available for only about one month, some roast a quantity of it and put it by for occasional use, so that it may last into the hot season.

Gabdagabda.—Both Fulani and Hausa make a food of this name from the young heads of bulrush-millet, which are stripped and put out to dry, and threshed by pounding. The threshed grain is put into boiling water and boiled until it is ' done ' to the extent of starting to split. Leaves of ' Indian hemp ' (Hibiscus cannabinus) are picked and put in, and boiled until cooked : if fresh butter is available, it is added ; also a little salt. The pot is taken off to cool and the food eaten, as a snack between meals. This is considered to be a strengthening food (as is mokokkorori), and is said to expel the weaknesses and aches and pains introduced by the wet season, such as the aching of the knee-joints—said to be caused by walking through dew-covered grass.

Mumandi (mumbri, a small portion).—The roasted grains of early bulrush-millet.

The above are, naturally, only available about the time of the bulrush-millet harvest.

Mbayundi.—A food made only by Fulani and eaten at weddings : is a dish of guinea-corn and beans cooked together, as made by some, or of guinea-corn only. Guinea-corn is threshed, and is pounded moist until clean and clear of husk (to this corn some add beans), as noted. Water is put in a pot and, when boiled, the unbroken guinea-corn is put in and boiled until cooked, then stirred, becoming like ' nyiri ' in substance, but with some unbroken grains in it, since some does not break down when thus cooked whole. It is stirred with fresh or clarified butter : some eat it as it is, others with fresh milk. It is only eaten at weddings, from custom : otherwise not eaten except perforce.

On the occasion of weddings, men, as a custom, cook meat in enormous quantities of butter ; but the result is said to be somewhat unpalatable.

Kurbo is a food given to women, after childbirth, to tone up the system and promote drainage from the womb. Such food may also be given to a person who has a chill : the practice is not confined to Fulani.

The food is prepared from the skin of the leg, below the knee and the hock, including the heel, and that from the muzzle or face (with the ears) where the skin is thick, of cattle ; with all the glutinous adherent flesh and membranes of these parts. The bone is removed and the hair singed and scraped off, when the meat is washed in hot water and boiled all day until tender. More water is then added ; small quantities of various peppers and spices are pounded, and mixed in, with pounded cake of fermented seeds of the locust-bean tree. Boiling is continued until the mass thickens, when the meat is removed. A little very fine meal is roasted until brown and added to this gravy as a thickening : the boiling mass is stirred until very thick.

This is given daily, if possible, from the day following childbirth until the seventh day after—the naming day of the child. It is then given again some four to seven days later, and once again during the next fortnight. If it is not possible to give 'kurbo', chicken meat with spices is given for the first week, while soups and (or) meat with spices, may be substituted for the 'kurbo' given during the following three weeks.

As a custom, among the Settled Fulani, on the fourth day after a birth, the relatives on the father's side, between themselves, buy and provide the ingredients, and take them to the home of the mother's parents, where they are cooked. This is in celebration of the birth : spices, cooked meats in which chicken predominates, and 'kurbo', being sent as presents to friends and relatives on this day. The nomads usually use a modified form of this food, including the lower leg and the 'heel', and broth.

Of the varieties given for the daytime meal, 'mbosiri' and 'chobbal' are by far the most commonly used, and one or other may be taken for a month or so without a change ; the others being used, by most, more by way of a change in the diet : it is not that more than one variety is made on any one day. The preparation of the food is in the hands of the women ; but the head of the family will inform them if he wishes to make a change in the food, or if he prefers or selects another food, to be eaten by the household.

Those such as 'ndinabari', which it is noticed are taken at about 9 or 10 a.m. (balte), are for the old and for the very young, who cannot wait until the time of the daytime meal, and for whom the normal foods of adults are unsuitable. 'Ndinabari' is considered very good for the old and for youngsters ; being strengthening, and the most useful of all foods to the body. Some then (at 9 or 10 a.m.) also partake of what will be eaten at the later 'kashitari'.

The salts used, apart from the European made salt ('manda kakanda'), are the salts 'manda baleha' (Kanuri 'mangul', Hausa 'bakin gishiri'), chiefly the variety commonly known as 'adabur'; 'manda mbodeha' (Hausa 'kantun gishiri') ; 'manda ndaneha' (Hausa 'beza'). Of the natrons, 'kanwa ndaneha' (white natron) is used in 'li'o polle' and similar soups in order to reduce the acidity ; 'kanwa mbodeha' (red natron) in 'mbosiri' (and is also drunk as a remedy for intestinal disorders).

Superstitious beliefs and prohibitions, rites and practices, abound among the Fulani, the degree varying in different sections : an attempt is made to cover the subject on broad lines.

There is a vast world of spirits, both benevolent and evil ones, known as 'hendu', plural 'keni'; 'ginnawol', plural 'ginnaji'; 'ginnol', plural 'ginni', also 'gwaigwaiji' (the Hausa gwaigwai), which exist round about us.

The name 'hendu, keni' is used in avoiding the use of the real names for spirits (which follow), just as the proper name for hyaena is often avoided.

Some spirits are said to exist in clouds, in rainbows, and in dust-devils or whirlwinds : others in old wells, which it is death to enter ; in water, in ruinous houses, and in unoccupied buildings : they are present in great numbers in large baobab and tamarind trees. There are spirits in nests of the grain collecting ant which, if interfered with, are said to cause illness, even if they do not cause a person to become mentally deranged : also in the nest of termites—although these, apparently, are less feared, some Fulani will not let their herdsmen or others knock down the termite hills.

Some spirits possess herds of wild animals. If the owner of livestock shoots one of these wild animals, the spirit or 'hendu' in charge will retaliate, and revenge itself by killing an animal, or animals, of the herd or flock—the word 'hendu' is among those applied to diseases which suddenly strike down cattle, such as Blackquarter—unless the owner has been successful in making a spell against the spirit before the spirit itself has made its spell : for spirits make spells, and if the spirit has made its spell before the stock-owner, the latter's will be of no avail. Did spirits not bind spells, they would not have the power of magically affecting persons and things, effected by casting a spell ovēr them.

These bowmen spirits (keni pidoji) are abroad at late night and about midday ; that is, at times when few people are about : all such spirits are to be feared at midday, as they 'shoot' persons coming out of bush at this time. They are also to be feared at night. Any affection for which there is no known cause, noticed in the morning, is said to be due to a 'pidowo jemma' or 'pidpiddo jemma', a "bowman of the night".

Spirits move away from places where people build or settle (though they may cause constant cracking of the walls of new buildings).

Nevertheless, certain Fulani, on moving to new ground, are so superstitious regarding them, that they light a fire in order to ascertain the presence or absence of spirits before making a new camp (hodde or hodirde). A preparation of the bark from a certain tree or shrub, pounded up, is put on a small fire, made when the air is still. If harmful spirits are present, the smoke of the fire goes straight up before spreading ; when another site, at some little distance, must be similarly tried out. If, however, the smoke from the fire drifts to some distance, at a little above ground level, before rising, it is an indication as to where the camp should be situated, and the Fulani move to, and camp, in that direction. The more orthodox Muhammadans regard this as superstitiousness and, as such, unnecessary.

Among the 'keni pidoji', 'Mallam Sambo' is a spirit to which is ascribed the sudden onset of disease which cannot be accounted for.

Certain 'keni' (cf. gwaigwaiji) further one's efforts to prosperity: they are of special value to cultivators, assisting them in the obtaining of a greater yield of corn; but one's individual helpful spirit must be propitiated and, if not given what one has promised, takes revenge by dispersing one's wealth. For example, they may be given a black calf or a black goat, which is slaughtered and offered up to the spirit.

It is almost needless to say that a staunch follower of Islam does not make them such offerings.

These 'keni' (gwaigwaiji) are said to be like very short men: they make weird noises likened by some to the crying of a cat or of a human being: they collect and converse at night. They can be seen at late night in towns, when few persons are astir, singly; but they collect in bush in numbers. They will wrestle with a man and, for all their smallness, throw him: should the man cry out, he will become mentally deranged: otherwise he flees unharmed from the spirit: it is said that actually very few persons do become mentally deranged on seeing 'gwaigwaiji', unlike seeing 'ginni', which are not like men in appearance, when mental derangement does then follow.

The two individual 'keni' to whom greatest credence appears to be given are 'Koriranwa' (maunirawa keni — the chief of the spirits), followed by 'Mallam Alhaji'. Apart from these are many other spirits named in 'bori'. All names of 'keni' are also known in Arabic.

Koriranwa can be seen clothed in white, and is very tall. A female spirit, she can at times be heard passing and calling her cattle along, being the possessor of a large number of cattle. While considered a relatively benign spirit, to Koriranwa is attributed paralysis of one side of the body; the cause of a withered arm or leg (the Hausa Inna or Doguwa), occasionally affecting the child in the womb, but more commonly later.

This spirit usually lives in a cavity under a rock; in the hollow of a baobab tree; or may dwell under a large tamarind; but always in bush where few people go. Should a number of people approach at one time, or too many in the course of one day, she will produce a crash, as of thunder, and frighten them away. Koriranwa is consulted as an oracle by Fulani; they have no other spirit to whom they apply for advice, and no spirit other than Koriranwa has an attendant.

Should a person wish to consult Koriranwa, he first approaches the attendant, who leads one to the oracle: he has a gourd in which gravel or small stones have been put, which he rattles to announce his approach, and advances to the abode of Koriranwa shouting out flatteries and praises. The supplicant pays his respects to her, but does not see her : she is said to speak in Fulani, receiving him with ; " Jabbama, jabbama " (welcome, welcome), so-and-so ; and after salutations have been exchanged, asks after the members of the family by name, and so on, without any intermediary or interpreter. One proffers one's request, and receives her answer of advice, direct. Cases in which an 'interpreter' puts his ear to a hollow, or to a hut, in which he affirms Koriranwa dwells, are spurious attempts to gain money, and only deceive the few, mainly women, who may believe the 'interpreter' when he tells them ; " Koriranwa says . . . "

Mallam Alhaji is a spirit 'cultivated' by persons seeking increase in wealth. To retain this spirit, a person has to keep with him white objects, such as a pure white sheep ; or white garments are put by, as Mallam Alhaji appreciates these objects.

Among followers or devotees of spirits, if it is suspected that there is a powerful spirit of value in a certain place, a number of devotees of the cult, from places in the adjacent areas, go to such spot and, being gathered together, each speaks in turn. He who is answered by the spirit is fortunate, for he becomes the attendant to the spirit (for example, attendant to Koriranwa of the Fulani) and will settle in a nearby village : to him will come those who wish to consult the spirit for remedies, advice and the like ; and, for his offices in taking them to the oracle, he will receive presents.

In connection with spirits is the subject of spirit possession. If spirits 'touch' a human being, he becomes possessed of spirits, or becomes a 'kenado'; or, if possessed by various spirits showing different symptoms, he or she is known as 'mo keni'. A spirit or 'hendu' wanders about, and returns to any one place in due course. It is fixed, or attached, to an area by giving it what it wants, so that it does not go far away from this place and, when summoned, will answer the call. Whatever actions the spirit goes through are imitated by the devotee or other person into whom it has entered : the actions of the person possessed (kenado or mo keni) are done by him in imitation of the character and doings of the spirt (hendu) ; that is, imitation becomes hysterical frenzy or 'hendu' ; (in Hausa 'bori'). Possession can be induced when required. It is largely practised by some of the Nomadic Fulani. A stringed musical instrument is one of the chief requirements in inducing the state. Different 'tunes' may be played on drums, during 'possession', for the various spirits. In other than 'bori' devotees, the desire is to get the person back to his senses, and not to 'raise' the spirit in him.

Should a person become affected by a spirit, he usually falls into a profound stupor : it is then necessary to discover the kind of spirit which has entered into him : this is done by exposing him to a fragrant smoke. When the type is discovered, the remedy can be applied. It consists of washing in certain concoctions made from tree-barks and the like, or binding an amulet (layaru) about the head ; as prescribed by one who practices magic (bokajo), or by a man of learning (modibbo), as the case may be ; and (or) with the addition of some herbal medicine in his food for the next several meals. After the first occasion, the articles necessary for the imitation of actions of the particular spirit are put by, in case the spirit should return on some future occasion.

Recovery is effected by sneezing: some, on getting up, at once sneeze and are recovered; others imitate the particular ' hendu ' for a short time, and then sneeze and recover. The spirit is then said to escape (that is, from among the people present).

The different spirits manifest themselves by different symptoms or actions, which are usually easily recognisable. A devotee may imitate more than one character or spirit, and the necessary ' properties ' are put by for use when required and the spirit possession induced. The particular spirit may be any one of a large number showing different manifestations, and the subject is far too large to be dealt with here in detail. Should the spirit of Koriranwa affect a Fulani, he walks out into bush calling cattle, like Koriranwa, and returns unharmed and recovered. A leather loin-wrap, ' waistcoat ' and plaited straw-hat, all heavily covered in cowries, is the appropriate attire for such. In some devotees in whom the spirit of Koriranwa is latent, the spirit may be aroused by a fiddle (gogeru) and, when manifested, the character of this spirit is acted, and the subject is able to give information, on being asked, as to cures, and the finding of things which have been lost, such as cattle and so on; which it is said the spirit of Koriranwa puts into his lips to say.

Should the spirit of Koriranwa or of Mallam Sambo affect a non-Fulani, he will speak in the Fulani tongue while under its influence.

Spirits may enter a person as a result of his having sat under a tree, or near some object; by the side of a river, or the like; in which, without his knowing it, there exists a spirit, whereby he becomes possessed.

After sunset,.following the evening devotions at that time, it is the custom to take a light or fire—even a glowing ember is sufficient—into each dwelling in which people will spend the night; so that spirits shall not remain in the dwelling, but shall be aware that humans are occupying it.

While ' kabbe ' expresses superstition or superstitious belief, ' mboda ' (pl. 'mbodaji') is — (i) — the knowledge or belief that by eating certain foods, doing certain things, meeting with certain objects; ill effect, ill luck or harm will follow: (ii)—the object that if eaten or met with, or the action that if performed; one knows or believes will be harmful, have ill effect or bring bad luck. The verb ' woda ' means—to know or to believe that by eating certain foods, doing certain things, meeting with certain objects; ill effect, ill luck or harm will follow.

Many ' mboda ' are peculiar to, and confined to, certain tribes. The following appear to be those more generally considered 'mboda'.

A blind person. To set out and meet with a blind person is unlucky: Fulani usually strike such a one with their staffs, and run off before he can strike them, to rid themselves of the ' mboda ': in vexing him they believe that they have passed on to him whatever vexation was in store for them. Conversely, it is lucky to meet a leper, who is given a present of alms in order that the luck may be increased.

To see a ground-squirrel (Xerus sp.), or a bandicoot (palm-rat), or a crested duiker, is unlucky ; but to see a red-fronted gazelle upon going out-of-doors in the morning prognosticates good luck.

The long pods of Cassia Kotschyana (and similar species) must not be brought into the home ; to do so is said to cause strife in the household. Poles of Combretum leonense must not be brought home for use as posts. The shrub Guiera senegalensis must not be burnt : note that the leaves and twigs are used for smudge-fires for the cattle.

Departure from one place to another should not be undertaken except on certain days of the lunar month : these vary with different tribes : the best days are said to be 7th, 17th, and 27th, though the 2nd, 4th and 9th are also days on which one might start a journey, work, etc. Various tribes exclude some of these days, or include others, and, especially in certain months, some avoid moving on certain days of the week.

Of the days of the week, Sunday, Tuesday and Friday are the days for catching and taking away, or for bringing, a beast which has been sold or bought : also for moving cattle. Friday is the best day of the week for moving, and for removal into a new home. Other days are not propitious for doing these things. Shaving of the head or beard should not be done except on a Monday or a Tuesday : if not on Monday afternoon, from about 4 p.m. onwards, then on Tuesday morning.

When misfortune befalls a person on a Wednesday it is likely to recur. One does not (go to) condole with a Fulani on a Wednesday on any loss he has sustained, or on the death of anyone in his household. (A present received on that day will lead to another following later on.)

A flaming torch or brand must not be brought into the house or shelter, but the ember blown into flame after one has entered. This appears to be general to Hausa peoples as well—perhaps a very practical prejudice. Some will not even allow a torch to flame in the open. Some will not bring wood or water into camp at night : some do not pound corn at night.

Branches and other obstacles should not be removed from the path : one should go round them. One reason given for this is that a man who habitually removes such obstructions will, if seeking a wife, always be outdone by a rival.

The true name of the hyaena (fouru) must not be uttered when a spell has been made against them, lest the spell (tiggere or renrude) be broken. There are some dozen alternative names for the hyaena which are used in avoiding the use of the proper name : such as ' ladderu' (creature of the bush), ' jemmaru ' (creature of the night), etc.

The entrance door to a hut or shelter should face West, or as near so as possible. If facing North, it is said that spirits will cause the occupier to leave the place for elsewhere, after but a comparatively short stay. If facing East, the occupants will never be free from sickness.

Some will not utter the word 'felmango', thunder-bolt or thunder-stroke, since it is used in an oath; "May I be struck dead by a thunder-stroke." —(compare with the Hausa 'aradu'): a word such as 'surango', meaning thunder, is substituted.

One must not step over the calf-tethering rope of another cattle-owner, lest something untoward affect his cattle: it is said that contact of the body of some individuals brings bad fortune.

One must not share the tongue of an animal; but eat the whole oneself; otherwise one will fall out with the person with whom it was shared.

An oxtail is not eaten, lest one's prosperity or wealth become reduced thereby. The tail being the part behind the rest of an animal's body, so will one become behind one's fellows in prosperity or wealth.

Certain tribes do not kill or eat of certain animals; for example, the red-fronted gazelle (lelwa); the land monitor or iguana lizard (futoru); the guinea-fowl (jaungal); the bush-fowl or francolin (gerlal); the snake (mbodi).

The majority of Fulani will not eat the fish known as 'kasu' lest leprosy, in the form of patches known as 'cheppam', appear on the body. There is said to be some flesh in the head—about the gills—which they 'woda'. Some (whose 'mboda' it is not, but who are nevertheless afraid of contracting 'cheppam'), take out this supposed evil part, since, if cooked with it, all the flesh will become tainted with it; but one with the 'mboda' will not even then partake of it, for fear that the evil principle has not been eradicated. Many others will not eat goat-flesh, said to be the best and richest of meat, and thence, if the person's body contains any disorder, such will be unmasked upon eating the meat: it is said that many an unhealthy state of the body develops into definite illness following the eating of goat-flesh. The above two 'mboda' are said to be inherited by children.

Individuals have their own personal 'mboda' regarding various foods, but these are not inherited by the children.

If fresh milk is spilt on the ground, it is considered, by many, as most unlucky: to remedy this, and avert ill-luck, hot water is poured on the spot. It is considered, by most, to be unlucky to sell fresh milk: they would prefer to make a present of it. It is of interest to note that the explorer Clapperton mentioned this in his journal in January, 1824, when referring to a somewhat romantic incident while travelling from the province of Katagum to Kano. The Wodabe do not share this 'mboda', since they throw away fresh milk surplus to the requirement of themselves and their milk-fed stock, and after giving some to their horses and dogs: they also sell fresh milk in the markets.

Fulani women, when retailing milk, are careful, before moving away, to draw the foot across the earth upon which the milk calabash—or the ring of bound grass on which it rested—has been set when measuring out milk for sale: in order that certain 'habe', some few of which are credited with the power, shall not be able to take up a little of the earth on which the calabash was placed, and effect a spell which will cause the milk-seller to spend the rest of the day without a customer.

Some combinations of hair colours (and certain other peculiarities) in a calf are considered very injurious ; such a calf is condemned by the elders, and is thrown away outside the camp, or into water, lest it have an evil effect on the herd. Others appear to take this ' mboda ' less seriously.

That some do believe in serious misfortune being due to certain hair coloration is shown in the following incident, which occurred a number of years ago in the town of Dakingari, in Gwandu Emirate. A fulani was being shaved, when he was told that a certain bull, exposed for sale in the market, had been bought and slaughtered. He asked which bull it was, and whether it was of such and such a colour. On being told that this was the bull, he ordered the barber to desist, and would not allow him to finish, saying that, before the shaving of his head were completed, there would be a cry of fire, which fire would result in a great conflagration : he clapped on his hat, and went off. Before he had left the place, a fire started, which eventually consumed practically the whole of the town. This was told me by another Fulani who was in the town at the time.

Other colours or peculiarities in a calf are considered to be lucky, and it may be decided that the calf be slaughtered in order that the blood may run in the cattle-penning place, while some of it is smeared over the owner's body, in order to procure increase in his cattle.

Butchers, not unnaturally, are connected with ill-luck, and are not welcome to work about the herd. A Fulani whom I have known for some years recently hinted to me, in all seriousness, that a larger mortality than he had been used to experience, following double-inoculation of his cattle against Rinderpest, was due to a butcher severing the flap of skin left uncut by the ear-punch used : (they insist that a butcher's knife be not used for this). On talking the matter over, he said that he would not argue that deaths were not due to some latent disease (Redwater had been seen) brought on following inoculation ; but I think this may have been politeness in deference to me.

It is the custom to apply certain prohibitions after a spell has been made, such as a spell against wild beasts (the prohibition against mentioning the true name of the hyaena has been mentioned), or against the disease 'hendu'. In one case, following the death of a beast, attributed to 'hendu', an elder who was consulted, and who bound a spell, gave instructions that no herding stick was to be thrown (a stick is sometimes thrown in order to turn a beast, or beasts, back) and all would be well. For several days all did go well, until a herd-boy, forgetting the instruction, threw his stick at a beast : on the following morning another beast was found dead : the spell had been broken. Most types of the Nomadic Fulani, if a spell has been made against 'hendu', do not allow black cloth or clothing to be worn by anyone coming, or working, among the cattle : many do not allow any person to mount a shelter (on the roof of which many of the impedimenta are usually kept) until such time as the danger has passed.

Spells and spell-binding are subjects of high importance in Fulani life. The word ' ayare ' (pl. ayaje), or ' harfere ', is used for 'a spell', from the verse or phrase from the Koran used in making a spell or charm. 'Kabbol' (a binding) is also used for 'a spell': 'habbugo ladde' is the binding of (the harmful things of) the bush.

A 'kabbol' may be obtained from one who practises magic—'ndarnowo' (or bokajo)—or from another Fulani, usually an elder.

An 'Ayare' is obtained only from a learned man (modibbo) well versed in the Koran. The 'ayare' plus spitting (mochugo) consititute the charm or spell. In charming away an injury or ache, a 'modibbo' will, after reading from the Koran, spit on the bunched fingers and apply them lightly to the part affected : or will use a charm to avert an evil, etc.

An applicant may obtain from a 'modibbo' either a paper on which the selected suitable words are written ; or may have the words repeated to him, and retain them in his memory, in order to make a spell of his own.

Such are not given indiscriminately to all and sundry, but to those who are considered to be responsible persons and who will not abuse their use. The type of 'ayare' will depend much on the purpose for which it is to be used, the 'modibbo' selecting the phrase or phrases, and informing the applicant that such are the words indicated : all 'ayaje' are taken from the Koran.

The jumble of words, incantation or magical formula, repeated by some as a means of warding off dangers, ill-luck, etc. (called jimdindirgo or jibindirgo) is, by many, including the more orthodox Muhammadans, considered as of little or no value as such, because no 'ayare' is used, merely "meaningless words which are like learning, but are not". However they concede that—since those who practise this form of spell and believe in such spells ; and since such forms, only, are within their knowledge and, being illiterate, they are not in a position to know other forms—God assists them in guarding themselves and their herds when they make these spells ; so that those who make them are not shamed before their followers : while, if they wrong God in making these spells, such will be settled on that day of the removal of all wrongs and injustices.

An 'ayare' (verse or phrase) which the possessor has memorised is recited and the spell spat onto the object to be used, or the paper on which the 'ayare' has been written may be used. One who is illiterate retains an 'ayare' in his memory.

A 'tiggere', plural 'tigge'; from the verb 'tigga'; is that which is set up or fixed, or planted in the ground ; for example, a stone on which the spell has been spat after incantation, or some other object which is buried ; or an object, such as a stick, which is fixed in position. Such 'tiggere' is in the form of chips, shreds or powder of the bark of various trees (ledde) and (or) of various other ingredients, which are put into an amulet (layaru), and are obtainable from those who practise magic, from other Fulani, or from hunters. An 'ayare tiggere' is an actual paper on which a verse or phrase from the Koran has been written by a 'modibbo', and which is buried.

A 'tiggere' or 'ayare tiggere' is used by a person settled in one place.

A ' renrude ', plural ' denrude ' ; from the verb ' rena ', to guard, look after, protect, watch over ; is an intangible spell, for which an ' ayare ' is recited and the spell is spat (' ayare renrude ' is the verse or phrase recited) : or, as mentioned above, a magical formula is repeated where no ' ayare ' is used. A ' renrude ' is used by one who is moving from place to place, since a nomad does not wish to leave his spell behind him : further, the effects of a ' tiggere '—in keeping beasts and birds of prey from the area in which it was employed—may continue for a considerable period after the nomad has moved on elsewhere. A person who is continually on the move would leave a number of ' protected ' areas over a wide field, and such beasts would still be unable to enter them. Since, then, wild animals against which the spell was made would be unable to obtain food in these areas, they would thereby be wronged, as they were created for a purpose and have their due rights.

Spells are used for protection against harm or damage, such as theft, or depredations by wild animals by night among livestock : to protect a certain area, such as a cattle-camp, compound or village, from harm.

If used for a harmful purpose, such as to injure another, and buried, such a spell is known as 'ure ' (connected with the verb 'uwa', to bury): this also may contain an 'ayare', or be composed of such ingredients as are comprised in the term 'ledde'. It is buried in some spot over which the intended victim is likely to pass. Following upon his stepping over it, serious swelling of the leg will occur, resulting in his being laid up for a long period : should some other person of the same name (of that family) step over it, his leg will swell to a less extent.

' Fidugo ' is the sending, by magical means, through the air, of some object to which the charm has been applied or attached, to ' strike ' a named victim at a distance, so as to cause his severe illness, if not his death. Blacksmith-made needles, boiled in a concoction of 'ledde', are put in fat of the black cobra 'chulendi', contained in a horn, until fat from the body of a dead person can be obtained, when it is rubbed onto the needles, with incantations : they are then ready for use. They are sent on their journey by blowing upon them, when they disappear on their errand. Cotton, collected from the boll when the wind is high, is also used, and is said to form a web which gradually covers all the area of the lungs, producing fits of coughing, which grow worse as the web extends, and from which recovery is very improbable.

'Noddandu feho', or 'noddugo feho', is the calling of the intended victim's name until his face is seen clearly reflected in a basin-(feho) of water into which powder of a prepared charm has been poured : a spear is plunged into the reflection, when blood will appear in the water : it will subsequently be learned that the victim is sick, and it is said that he usually dies a short time afterwards.

Other methods include : to collect a number of ' modibbe ' to recite the Chapter of Y.S. (Ya Sin) from the Koran while a cockerel is killed in the name of the intended victim, when it is loosed to flutter and leap about before it dies ; in order to encompass the death, after

‘ induced ’ madness, of a person : to take chippings of certain barks and throw them into an old well, after ‘ preparation ’; in order that a named victim may long linger in sickness : to kill, and leave to rot, a skink (also after ‘ preparation ’) ; so that the victim may contract the ‘ cheppam ’ form of leprosy.

‘ Sokugo ’ ; from the verb ‘ soka ’, to wander, wander aimlessly, wander from or leave one’s home or country ; consists of making a charm from secret ingredients (ledde), or from an ‘ ayare ’, so that a person in his (otherwise) full senses leaves a place of his own will : an office-holder renounces his office or rulership under its influence, and departs. It is said that Fulani, more than any others, practise this form of charm. A favourite method is to tie an amulet (layaru), containing the charm, to the neck of a dove, which alights on the person’s house : it then flies off, he following to wherever it may go. Too late he will realise that he has been charmed away, his office by that time having been filled.

The ‘ magical means ’ and incantations used in affecting a person at a distance come under the general term of ‘ hubago ’. A person who possesses an antidote (known as rena hore) will escape all effects of ‘ hubago ’.

The secret of a spell is kept closely by the possessor. In all probability a man will not tell even his sons of the particular spell or spells he uses : he may tell a well-trusted son, lest the secret of the spell be lost. To try and make use of another’s charm is useless, except the possessor of the secret has been asked for, and has freely given, the recipe.

When making a spell to safeguard a certain area, the maker will repeat in his mind the area which he wishes to guard (for example, “ I purpose to guard my home ”) and (or) the period for which he wishes the spell to remain active. A spell is at first very strong, and will probably cover the nearby surrounding area for some time ; but gradually weakens.

A spell may be repeated nightly before retiring ; but in such a ‘ day-to-day ’ spell there is the danger of forgetting it for a night, when the cattle, or whatever else it is designed to guard, will remain unprotected for that night. A one-day spell, probably entailing some prohibition on the maker, may be made for such purposes as recovery of an animal which has strayed or become lost. A ‘ modibbo’, depending on such things as his learning and faith, may make a spell of very long duration. Periods of 40 days, 40 months, or 40 years are spoken of. The breaking of a condition or prohibition will break the ‘ tiggere ’ and ‘ renrude ’ spells.

A form of charm (of the type included under the term ‘ habbugo ladde ’) may be made for the recovery of an article which has been lost, ensuring that no one will approach the spot, or see the article, except the owner or those searching for it on his behalf. A phrase is repeated and a knot made in a certain object : some use the sinew of a monkey ; some a strip of the skin of the ‘ barkehi ’ (Bauhinia reticulata or ‘ bark bush) ’. Some use the dung of the crown-bird in making such spells. The spell is spat onto the object used.

Charms can be made to prevent animals from straying, to cure headache, toothache, and many ills and injuries.

' Ronga ' is a power of affecting persons or things by magical means, or of casting a spell over them. Many ' ronga ' appertain to the head.

A ' ronga ' may be made, or it may be a natural quality. It may be made from ' ledde ' supplied by those who practise magic, or of written 'ayaje'. Older men, especially, wear such a spell in their caps, to protect the head : should a person touch the cap, or attempt to remove it, or give the wearer a slap on the head, he is instantly stunned and falls down in a state of collapse. When applying such a 'ronga', the possessor will specify exceptions to whom the harmful influence is not to apply ; for example, children, who know no better and may touch the head in play ; and especially the grandchild, who is allowed special licence with the grandfather by custom of ' sidosido ' or ' wannyo-wannyo '.

Twins possess a natural power of 'ronga'. It is said that if only one of twins possesses it, the other will either die or be always ailing.

The most usual characteristic of this power in twins is that one who insults, curses, or seriously annoys them, will be stung by a scorpion. In some cases a snake may replace the scorpion, or the person will be involved in some law-case to his great disadvantage.

The scorpion has not the power to sting such twins, who also have the power of charming away the effects of a scorpion sting in another by rubbing the part affected.

To reduce their supposed magical powers, 'bakke', fragments of food which have stuck to the cooking-pot, are put into the bed of young twins : if they eat the fragments, the power is broken.

Among animals and birds, there is a ' ronga ' in the head of the road antelope, the hyaena and the duiker.

Certain eagles (Gyps ruppellii or Ruppell's griffon) and certain vultures possess such powers to some extent. The crown-bird is also credited with such powers. While I was at Bendu, in Gwandu Emirate, a year or two ago, a man who interested himself in catching such eagles (whose feathers, skin and bones are used in a variety of charms) is said to have died as the result of an eagle's 'ronga'. He trapped one bird, which escaped : the following day he trapped the same bird, and this time killed it, near the village ; but was himself at once struck down : parts of his body (his testicles) swelled up alarmingly, and he was soon near to dying ; both man and bird were carried into the village dead.

The duiker is credited with many magical qualities. Should anyone touch the head of a crested duiker, he will become possessed and behave like a madman : the hand which touched the crest may be put into fire to purify it, and so rid the person of the ' hendu ' or evil spirit which has entered into him. Should anyone shoot the animal, even though the bowman himself does not become demented, his child may become so. If a woman in child touches the crest of the duiker, these natural spirits (padde), should they not cause her to become demented, will bring about her giving birth to a child subject to fits from which, if it does not fall with some part of the body in a fire, it will take long to recover : if, however, it falls with, for instance, a hand in the fire, recovery quickly follows : in either case, however, the fits will recur at intervals.

Note that, in contrast, a woman in child, who has been able to touch, or to stroke, the red-fronted gazelle (Gazelle rufifrons), or even if she has seen one during her pregnancy, will produce a fine looking child.

Some say that if a cow strides across the standard-winged night-jar, her udder will swell up for three days, during which time her milk will be bad : if a man, his testicles will swell for the same period.

The constituents of a charm conferring the power of becoming invisible (sairudu) are often enclosed in pieces of the skin of the foetus of a duiker.

A belief that trees and shrubs with a milky sap, for example the figs, will increase cattle numbers and the milk - yield of cows, leads to the use of such by owners ; the bark may be pounded, and a concoction drunk by the cattle-owner : or very early morning washing of the body in such a concoction is favoured, often with the addition of a charm obtained from a 'modibbo'. Such a charm is written by the 'modibbo' on a writing-board. The writing is washed off with water into a calabash, and poured from this into the cattle-owner's bottle-gourd, which he takes home with him. Such a charm is often sprinkled onto the salts given to cattle for a lick. The parasitic shrub 'sotore' (Loranthus pentagona, etc.) is often pounded and mixed in.

It is customary to spread the natron or salt for cattle on a termite hill—cattle may often be observed to be gnawing at the earth of such ; the theory being that, as a termite hill is constantly gradually increasing in size, so will the cattle increase in numbers : if a termite hill is knocked away it will again be built up, so, should a herd meet with a decimating disease, in like manner will it grow again.

A number of Fulani believe that various means can be employed which will cause their cows to produce heifer calves. Among certain of them who pass through the Wase area when moving to other grazing grounds there is said to be a 'spirit' bull which lives on the inaccessible top of the tall, precipitous Wase rock, near the summit of which the Fulani aver there is a considerable pool of clear water. The bull is said to beget heifer calves, and to descend to the sandy plain at the foot of the rock on Thursday and Friday nights : all cows and heifers which he mounts on these nights will produce heifer calves.

For this reason, these Fulani, when passing near the rock on their way to the Taraba River grazing, bring their cattle (or used to do so, for the custom appears to be falling into disuse) to the foot of the rock for these two nights and, having hobbled them, leave them for the night untended, continuing their journey on the Saturday morning. The legendary bull, being a ' spirit', does not, of course, age with the passing of time. It is confidently stated that it has been seen on various occasions.

Also in the Wase area is a pool which never dries up : it is almost an arm of the river, though it does not apparently actually connect with it. In this pool, also, is said to be a bull endowed with similar powers, which emerges only at nights, and mounts cows and heifers hobbled nearby.

A method of determining what should be one's ' lucky colour ' in domestic animals, before recommencing to build up one's livestock, after having experienced the loss of one's herd through disease, is to make a trial with ' Bambarra groundnnts ' (Voandzeia subterranea). The seeds of these plants are of various colours ; white, blackish, reddish or brown, and speckled or mottled. A number of seeds, comprising one of each of the various colours which the person making the test can obtain, are sown closely together, but no one seed lying upon another, in earth contained in a gourd, or in a small patch of earth, and the earth watered.

When the seedlings have come up, it will be found that after four to seven days one of them will have outgrown the others considerably, being more vigorous in growth. The earth is carefully eased way until the seed of that plant is exposed and its colour can be seen, and upon this will depend the colour of the stock which the experimenter will purchase in order to refound his fortunes—whether it be a hen, a goat or a heifer— as this has been shown by the trial to be the colour favourable to his fortunes and indicative of the stock which he will in future maintain.

' Surnugo '—exposing to a frangrant smoke—has been mentioned in connection with the smudge-fires lighted at the cattle resting-place.

There is a certain charm made to ensure the return of cattle to their resting-place : this is put onto and among the twigs of the ' geloki ' (Guiera senegalensis), the leaves of which are those used for ' surnugo ' of cattle. This charm must be repeated at each new camp.

Yet another charm is used to prevent thieves or other unauthorised persons taking an owner's cattle. It has the effect of making the cattle lie down rather than follow or be dragged away. When making the spell, the maker will specify the persons to whom it does not apply ; for example, himself, his younger brother, etc.

' Harfindirgo ' is the effecting of a charm which will prevent a person remaining in a certain place, and make it impossible for him to spend even a day there without severe sickness or some grievous trouble afflicting him ; or to bring him into great disfavour ; or to get an office-holder into disfavour so that one may get a chance to usurp his position. It is said that, should such a charm be worked between a certain person and certain cattle, they will attack him at sight and kill him.

To bring one into prominence, as a man among men and, so, for selecting as a leading man, the skin of the forehead of a hyaena is highly prized.

Certain spells to harm a person require the inclusion of an object personal to him, such as hair cuttings (which are buried to prevent this), a piece of one of his garments, etc.

The making of charms constituted from various tree-barks and other objects is almost unlimited. Likewise, a booklet could be written on the various remedies and potions which are extracted from plants alone : these are usually a secret to the possessor of the knowledge. Certain men have a most extensive knowledge of this herbal lore, and I have found it most interesting to cover a patch of ground with one of these whose confidence I have, and be told of the uses to which the various herbs and shrubs may be put. Naturally, remedies and charms vary considerably in composition, and one can at times acquire a few of the ' secrets ' of one tribe from a member of another and, so, vice versa ; but rarely direct.

Chiefly Fulani. H. indicates a Hausa word ; A. indicates Arabic or of Arabic origin ; K. indicates Kanuri. Some words not marked are commonly used by Fulani, though they are not of Fulani origin.

adabur. A variety of manda baleha.

aradu. (H). Thunder-bolt, thunder-stroke. Cf. felmango.

ardo. A Fulani chief or leader.

ayare, pl. ayaje. A verse or phrase from the Koran ; used to denote 'a spell'. Cf. harfere.

ayare renrude. A phrase from the Koran recited for a renrude spell.

ayare tiggere. A paper on which a phrase from the Koran is written : buried for a 'fixed' spell tiggere.

Ba'en. A Fulani tribe.

Bagananko'en. A Fulani tribe.

bakin gishiri. (H). *See* manda baleha.

bakke. Fragments of food which have stuck to the cooking-pot.

balma. A salt included in manda mbodeha.

balte. 9 to 10 a.m.

bangal. Marriage.

Barebari. A Kanuri.

barkehi. The shrub Bauhinia reticulata.

Barno Nguddiri. The area Hadejia, Katagum, Misau Jama'ari.

belbel. Poor quality white butter, being adulterated with a quantity of butter-milk.

beza. (H). Cf. manda ndaneha.

Bodado. A member of the Fulani tribe Wodabe.

bokajo. One who practices magic. Cf. ndarnowo.

bori. (H). Hysterical frenzy.

bulude. The grasses Pennisetum pedicellatum and P. setosum.

burburwa. (H). A grass. *See* saraji.

burugu. (H). The grass Panicum stagninum.

chelbi. The grass Aristida Sieberiana.

cheppam. A form of leprosy.

chobbal. A food. Id. H. fura.

chofal. A tribute (now a tax) payable on cattle. Also known as jangal (H. jangali).

chulendi. A black cobra.

dakkere. A food.

dalli. A palm. Phoenix reclinata (?).

danidam. Id. nyallunde. Whole milk curdled, for use as mburwadam or for churning.

datanniya. (H). A grass. Id. kagarakagumji (K)., which *see.*

datsi. (H). The grass chelbi.

daye. A spring of young grass.

diyya. (A). Compensation for relatives of the person killed in a case of manslaughter.

docchal. A remainder or remnant. A term used for the Rinderpest outbreak of 1919-20.

Doguwa. (H). A spirit said to cause paralysis of one side of the body.

dumirde. A wet season cattle-camp.

Fatiha. (A). Phrase from the Koran read or repeated at a marriage ceremony. (The Opening Chapter of the Koran.)

feho. An earthenware basin.

felmango. Thunder-bolt or thunder-stroke.

fidugo. Sending by magical means an object, to which a charm has been applied, to strike down a victim at a distance.

fijirde dampe. A widely popular Fulani dance.

foga. A salt included in manda mbodeha.

fouru. A hyaena. The true name of the hyaena.

Fulbe. Pl. of Pullo, which *see*. Fulani people : the Fulani.

Fulfulde. The Fulani language.

furei. (H). The grass saraji.

futoru. Land monitor or iguana lizard.

gabdagabda. A food.

gabdi. The tree Acacia arabica.

gamagari. (H). Name used for the Rinderpest outbreak of 1913-14.

Gambaraji. A type of cattle evolved by crossing White Kano with local red cattle of marshes of Yauri Emirate.

garlabal. The grass Andropogon (Arthrolepis).

geloki. The shrub Guiera senegalensis.

gerewol. A dance of the sections of the Wodabe group.

gerlal. A bushfowl or francolin.

ginnawol, pl. ginnaji. A spirit. Cf. hendu.

ginnol, pl. ginni. A spirit. Cf. hendu.

Gobirawa. (H). The Gobir people : a warlike Hausa people whose chief had decreed the extermination of the Fulani (a.d. 1804).

gogeru. A fiddle.

golombi. The tree Stereospermum Kunthianum.

gubuwol. The plant Vitis pallida.

gulutche. Skimmed sour milk.

gwaigwaiji. (pl). Cf. H. gwaigwai. Spirits said to resemble short men.

habbugo ladde. A binding of (the harmful things of) the bush.

hako polle. *See* li'o polle.

haram. (A). Utterly forbidden.

harfere. A verse or phrase from the Koran : used to denote a 'spell'. Cf. ayare.

harfindirgo. Effecting a charm in order to get a person into disfavour, or to ensure that evil befall him if he remains in a certain place.

harkiya. (H). The grass morsollo.

hendu, pl. keni. The hidden name for spirits, benevolent and evil. 2. A name for disease which suddenly strikes down cattle (etc.) : includes Anthrax, Blackquarter : Cf. Ladde. 3. Hysterical frenzy.

hodde. A temporary cattle-camp. (Also hodirde).

hoggo. The cattle resting-place at a camp, where the cattle spend the night. Id. walde.

hubago. A general term for the magical means, incantations, used to affect a person at a distance.

ibbi. The tree Ficus gnaphalocarpa.

iddat. (A). The period of continence for a widow or divorcee before she may remarry.

Id el Fitr. (A). The festival at the end of the fast month Ramadan. (That is, on the first day of Shawal.)

Id el Kabir. (A). The festival on the tenth day of Zul hajji.

Inna. (H). Id. doguwa. Cf. Koriranwa.

jabbama. " Welcome ", in salutation to a visitor.

Jabtoji. A type or breed of red long-horned cattle.

Jafun Fulani. A Fulani tribe ; the Jafun'en.

jaungal. A guinea-fowl.

" Jeda, inna ma wartai." " Be quiet, your mother will come back."

jelgol. Marking of calves' ears with a knife.

jelgol chumal. Marking by branding with a hot-iron.

jemmaru. A name for the hyaena, used to avoid mentioning its proper name fouru. Cf. with ladderu.

jibindirgo. An incantation or magical formula.

jimdindirgo. Id. jibindirgo.

jonte. *See* pabboje.

Julde Laiha. The festival of Id el Kabir.

Julde Sumaye. The festival of Id el Fitr.

kabbe. Superstition : superstitious belief.

kabbol. A ' spell '.

kado, pl. habe. A non-Fulani native.

kagarakagumji. (K)., used by Fulani. The grass Thelepogon elegans.

kahi. The tree Khaya senegalensis.

kalgo. (H). The shrub barkehi.

kamsuwa. (H). The grass bulude.

kantun gishiri. (H). *See* manda mbodeha.

kanwa mbodeha. Red natron.

kanwa ndaneha. White natron.

karairayau. (H). The grass garlabal.

karan kabau. (H). The grass garlabal.

kashitari. Main morning meal, properly taken at 11 a.m.—12 noon. Id. mbottari.

kasu. A fish not eaten by the majority of Fulani owing to a ' mboda ' regarding it.

kawirabe. Pl. Maternal uncles.

kawohi. The Hausa kawo. The tree Afzelia africana.

kenado. One possessed by a spirit.

keni pidoji. Pl. ' Bowmen ' spirits.

Keteji. The almost humpless cattle of the Borgu Fulani.

kewe. Pl. Bamboos — Oxytenanthera abyssinica.

kirtari. Evening meal.

koggal. Custom of betrothal of young children.

Koriranwa. The chief of the Fulani spirits ; a female spirit consulted as an oracle. (Koriranwa maunirawa keni.)

kunuri. The Hausa kunu. A gruel. Cf. mbosiri.

kurbo. A food given after childbirth.

ladde. A term applied to diseases which suddenly strike down cattle—as Blackquarter.

ladderu. A name for the hyaena, used to avoid using its proper name fouru. Cf. with jemmaru.

lafolafo. Striking of a ' comrade ' by another under the custom of ' relationship in play '.

layaru. An amulet.

ledde. Chips, shreds, or powder of the bark of various trees, used in some spells.

leggel bali. A shrub readily eaten by ruminants.

lelwa. A red-fronted gazelle.

li'o. Soup or gravy.

li'o bokki. Soup or gravy made with baobab leaves.

li'o kubeje. ,, ,, okra.

li'o polle. ,, ,, red sorrel leaves. Id. hako polle.

Mallam Alhaji. The name of a spirit.

Mallam Sambo. The name of a spirit to which is ascribed a sudden onset of disease which cannot be accounted for ; one of the ' keni pidoji '.

manda baleha. A dark native salt. Cf. bakin gishiri ; mangul.

,, kakanda. European-made salt.

,, mbodeha. A red na ive salt.

,, ndaneha. A whitish native salt. Cf. H. beza.

mangul. (K). A salt included in manda baleha.

maudo wuro. The senior male Fulani of a camp or settlement.

mbafu. Dry leaves of guinea-corn.

mbayundi. A food eaten at weddings.

mboda, pl. mbodaji. A belief in harm arising from certain things. 2. The objects from which harm may arise. Verb woda. For full definition *see* text.

mbodi. A snake.

mbordam. A food.

mbosiri. A gruel. Id. kunuri.

mbosiri tainandi. Thin watery mbosiri.

mbottari. The main morning meal, properly taken at 11 a.m. to 12 noon. Id. kashitari.

mburwadam. Whole milk which has been curdled, to be used for whisking.

mochugo. Spitting (in connection with making a spell or charm).

modibbo, pl. modibbe. Learned man : man of letters : teacher.

mo keni. One possessed by various spirits.

mokokkorori. A food.

mordi babdi. A highly ornamental style of hairdressing for a woman prior to return to her husband after her first child-bearing.

morsollo. The grass Digitaria debilis.

Muharram. (A). The first month of the Muhammadan year.

mumandi. Roasted grains of early bulrush-millet : (mumbri=a small portion).

ndarnowo. One who practises magic. Cf. bokajo.

ndinabari. A food.

ndiyam kewe. Waters in or by which the bamboo kewe abounds.

ngajiri. A form of nyiri made in East Hausa—the Kanuri form of nyiri.

ngari koggal. A bull given by the boy's father to the girl's father as sealing the agreement of a ' koggal ' betrothal (*see* koggal).

ngewari koye. Break fast (lit.).

njonkadam. Sour buttel-milk. Id. pendidam.

njuggam. Sour butter-milk put by specially for souring the next day's milk.

njulandi. Pulp of baobab fruits.

njutari. A component of mbosiri (which *see*), made separately and turned into the mbosiri.

noddandu feho. Calling a person's name in order to spear the reflection of his face supposedly seen in water magically prepared in a basin, so that the distant victim shall fall sick and die.

noddugo feho. Id. noddandu feho.

nyaile. Stubble-grazing over farms after harvest.

nyallunde. Whole milk curdled for use as mburwadam or for churning. Id. danidam.

nyamri. A food.

nyiri. = nyiri unandi. A porridge taken with soup or gravy: the Hausa tuwo.

nyiri takkirde = ngajiri.

oppere, pl. oppe. Feverishness.

" O yari pulaku mako." " She has kept her virginity."

pabboje. Fulani sickness: typically a headache every other day only, of four to fourteen days duration, at harvest time. Cf. jonte.

padde. Natural—as opposed to induced—spirits.

paturi. A food of Nomadic Fulani herdsmen.

pendidam. Sour butter-milk. Id. njonkadam.

pidowo jemma. A " bowman of the night "; a spirit to which is said to be due any affection, noticed in the morning, for which there is no known cause.

pidpiddo jemma. Id. pidowo jemma.

pulaku. Fulani code of conduct. Fortitude under pain, or in adversity.

Pullo, pl. Fulbe. A Fulani.

Rahaji clan. A Fulani clan, the Rahajinko'en.

rena hore. Antidote to (charms under) ' hubago '.

renrude, pl. denrude. An intangible spell, not ' fixed '; used by one moving from place to place, to protect property, etc. Verb rena.

ronga. A power of affecting persons or things by magical means, such ' ronga ' often appertaining to the head, and may be man-made or be a natural quality.

sairudu. A charm conferring the power of becoming invisible.

sammore. A term which includes Trypanosomiasis.

sannu. Used as a term for the Rinderpest outbreak of 1887-91; from the Hausa greeting, or term of commiseration.

saraji. The grass Eragrostis tremula.

sedirde. A dry season cattle-camp.

sendugo jaudi. Distribution of property, estate (of a deceased person).

seto. ' Tornado season '; the hot season just before the rains set in.

shanganehi. The tree Ficus iteophylla.

shannehi. The tree Ficus kawuri.

sidosido. Playing of tricks on one another by ' comrades ' under the custom of ' relationship in play '.

Sirati'en. Kanuri. Cf. Barebari.

" Soinde na'i." Lack of, paucity of, cattle.

sokugo. A charm to cause a person to leave his home, office, etc. abandon his rulership. Verb soka.

sollungo. Inter-seasonal period when guinea-corn is ripe, just before the cold dry season.

soro. A Fulani game—test of self-control.

sotore. Loranthus pentagona (etc.).

surango. Thunder.

surnugo. Exposing to a fragrant smoke.

takkirde. A steamer for cooking food by steaming.

tamsere. Cakes of flour of guinea-corn or bulrush-millet cooked in oil or butter (the Hausa waina or masa), or of wheatmeal, or wheatmeal and beanmeal, or beanmeal and guinea-corn flour (the Hausa pinkaso or algaragi).

tiggere, pl. tigge. A ' fixed ' spell used by a person settled at one place, to protect property, etc.

ure. A spell buried in order to harm a certain individual. Verb uwa.

ushira. (A). ' Estate duties '.

walde. The cattle resting-place at a camp, where they spend the night. Id. hoggo.

wannyowannyo. Id. sidosido.

woda. To have a belief that harm arises from certain things. The verb connected with mboda, which *see*.

Wodabe. A Fulani tribe or clan.

wodebe. People with red (brown) skin: hence, Europeans. Sing = bodejo.

wurwa. To whisk.

Yankanaji. ' White Kano ' type cattle.

yamnde. Time of guinea-corn harvest.

Ya Sin. The chapter Y.S. of the Koran.

zakat. (A). A religious offering. Locally = zakka.

zazzabi. (H). Feverishness : *see* oppere.

zura. Mid-afternoon.